Truth about Bodybuilding Supplements

"This is a five star book that gives you facts about supplements you must know to be a professional bodybuilder. It is new, the only and most comprehensive."

Vlastimil Slechta,
Qualified for English Championship Finals
(see his picture on the book cover)

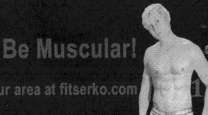

"I dedicate this book to Charlie, a regular goer to the Virgin Active gym in Chelmsford and a fitness model whose outstanding physique and presence in the gym motivated me to dedicate my business to Bodybuilding.

Thank you, Charlie"

Serge Kolpa

TABLE OF CONTENTS

DISCLAIMER

Before taking any advice from this book, obtain the advice of a licensed medical professional. The intent of the book is to provide some health information to help you with any health specialist you choose to advise you. Health, medical, dietary and exercise fields of expertise are widely divergent in viewpoints.

Before implementing any advice from this book it is recommended to consult a licensed medical professional, if you do not consult a licensed medical professional you are self prescribing; hence the author or any party involved do not assume any responsibility for what you do after you review this book or any part of it.

Be warned you are solely responsible for how you use supplements discussed in this book, the author or any other party involved are not responsible for any consequences or any damages claimed against them. The recommendations made in the book are opinions formed by the author to the best of his knowledge at the time of writing the book.

Information in this book does not intend to nor attempt to, prescribe against, diagnose, cure, prevent or treat any disease or illness. It is necessary that the readers of the book are, before acting upon any information within the book, healthy, free of disease and or illness.

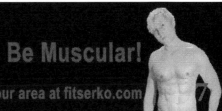

INTRODUCTION

I remember when I began to use fitness supplements, it was when I was ill informed of them. While surfing online or visiting a store, I was just paralyzed by indecision. I would search online for hours to figure out supplements, but without finding any definite results. In fact, I would be more confused at the end of the search.

There are so many different branded supplements and marketing gimmicks that you cannot trust a shop assistant who overloads you with hype and misinformation. Because of this confusion, I used to buy the most expensive supplement, which claimed to make one buff in the shortest amount of time. The hype of supplements made them appear to be almost illegal and I thought this was the reason for its high effectiveness. I logically thought that the supplement's high price and popularity must be because of its miraculous results.

Years later, I became experienced and I researched the ingredients of supplements and understood them. Over the years, I have met many bodybuilders who are real fitness models for magazines, calendars and clothing companies. Their advice and guidance has improved my understanding of supplements. My suspicions were confirmed that many of the expensive supplements were just expensive overhyped junk. I could

have spent a couple of holidays abroad in the sun for the money I spent on supplements.

Nowadays, when I shop for supplements retail assistants dislike me because when they approach me to relieve me of my hard earned cash for overpriced, overhyped useless junk, I show them that I am more knowledgeable than them and I will not be taken for a ride.

Some shop assistants approach me for advice as soon as they see my strong physique. As you might have guessed, summer is my favorite season of the year because I can wear tight vests to show off my strong physique.

Through years of experience and fitness achievements, I have gained a wholesome picture of supplements. Now, I am in a position to help you to save money and, most importantly, help you to stop squandering years of your life in trying different supplements.

I must warn you that if you want to become buff the supplements by themselves will not help you achieve this goal. You must also have a great fitness routine and healthy lifestyle. Well-designed gym exercises are significantly more effective than any supplement. However, with the correct

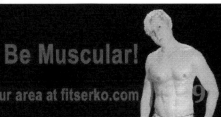

knowledge and application of fitness supplements, you can speed up your program's progress and proudly admire your own body in the mirror.

Truth about Bodybuilding Supplements

Only for Professional Bodybuilders

BODYBUILDING SUPPLEMENTS' LIES

While we are buying anything, we might think that our decision is logical, but, in reality, we buy emotionally and then we justify the purchase through logic.

Many people have experienced this situation. Arriving at a supplement store, you notice the buffed-up bodybuilders on labels of supplements and, instantly, you want to become like them. Next, you think of reasons or excuses to buy the specific supplement. Your excitement rises further if a label advertises the supplement's "medical virtues" which you trust. Alternatively, the supplement's dark colors give it a trendy appearance, so you think it is almost illegal and it must work.

After thoroughly reading the label you ask for help from a retail assistant who, in most cases, is not your helper as he will confirm whatever you want to hear. If it is expensive you feel a gag in your throat, but you want to become buff. Even if it is too expensive for your budget, you feel somewhat humiliated, especially if anyone else is around to judge you.

On top of that, a retail assistant has just spent his time answering your questions. This makes you feel guilty for wasting their time, but, in reality, it is their job to provide an answer for your questions! Next, you feel so

embarrassed because of the retail assistant's stares that you suddenly develop the quality of telepathy and you can hear him clearly say: "If you cannot afford it, then don't waste my time. You are a looser because you don't have enough money to buy it!"

To add more to the mental torture, someone just bought a large quantity of those expensive supplements. This only increased your feelings of inferiority. In the hope of an escape, you shift to another shelf with cheaper products. You refuse to leave the store because you cannot admit a complete defeat.

You can still sense the retail assistant's stare on your back. You can hear him talk to a colleague and they laugh together. Somehow you are completely sure that they laughing at you. In the end, you buy a cheaper supplement with your clouded mind, pretending you found your ideal supplement, but you still you feel horrible inside. You believe that, because it is cheaper, it is less effective.

You feel defeated and eventually browse online for solutions where small and big scammers market their products. Their marketing entices you buy into more fitness frauds. However, you never discover the ideal supplement. In spite of that, because you read so much and someone

sponsored by fitness companies advised you, you think that you made the right choice. Sounds familiar?

There are thousands of different supplements and brands. It is hard for supplement companies to fight for the number one position. They know that we are highly emotional creatures, so they appeal to this characteristic. They create an excitement with the marketing of their products.

Just look at Apple's secret releases of their iPads, iPhones, Macbooks and iMacs. Thousands of Apple fans queue to get their hands on the new products on the day of release and they pay premium prices compared to other brands. Have you ever seen Apple fans being excited and hyped up by retail assistants with gestures and cheers? I think Apple looks like a cult when its staff excites their customers. I do not observe many differences between religious marketing and Apple's marketing.

Branding is a very effective marketing tool. It personalizes a company and provides an edge over other competitors in the market. It ensures the brand loyalty; if you bought a supplement from company X and hoped it worked, why should you buy a supplement from company Z? They want you to pay them regularly over the period of your entire life. Often, they make ridiculous claims to grab your attention and make you believe in a false, rosy, unreal world.

Suddenly a simple Vitamin complex with a small amount of caffeine and pepper becomes a super fat burner. Alternatively, a mixture of Zinc, Vitamin B6 and Calcium will give you the physique of a movie star by raising you testosterone levels to barely legal levels. Some products main ingredients are just Caffeine and Vitamins B. Some of the product companies claim to have a closely guarded secret formula. Yes, I guess the secret is that there is no secret.

In the world of supplements, this practice is very convenient. It is not the same as buying a car, which simply does not work. It is not easy to disapprove their claims. They claim that they have studies, which prove their supplements work because they contain all of the amino acids (also known as protein e.g. chicken meat). Amino acids have been proved to be essential for muscle growth. It is like saying water is a miracle supplement because it hydrates and without it performance is drastically worsened. It is too easy to carry out unscrupulous marketing and it is too tempting when repercussions are very unlikely.

Marketing works and this is why senior marketing executives are highly paid. Companies would not spend money on advertising and marketing strategies and tactics if they waste time and resources. Ask yourself: if you saw your favorite buff movie star endorsing a supplement would you buy it? Would you buy another supplement if it is just powder in a plastic pouch

Truth about Bodybuilding Supplements
Only for Professional Bodybuilders

and has a very high price tag on it? Unless it was steroids and you believed in its effectiveness, I am guessing you would not buy it.

Nevertheless, do not feel hopeless about yourself. There are good, explainable reasons for our behavior. In short, with the abundance of available information on supplements, we want reliable information, so we trust the "well-informed" choices of our heroes; we create stereotypes of people and the reliability of labels based on appearance. If we analyzed every minute detail, we would not progress and we would be completely paralyzed with indecision.

We are not only targeted through shops and over the Internet, fitness magazines virtually make you thirsty for a great shape by presenting fitness models and other successful looking men. At the same time, they quietly suggest a particular supplement that will hardly help you to reach your sought after physique.

Sometimes, fitness companies offer a "free" fitness program with a minimal amount of coaching and monitoring through the Internet. However, if you are committed to their program it will cost you an astonishing amount of money to buy their products. Similarly, fitness companies also exhibit film stars and encourage you to download their star workout free, accompanied with a staggeringly expensive nutrition plan.

Another trick that you have to be aware of is the claims of super results, based on dubious research, by companies. Some time ago, I produced my dissertation at the University of Essex in the UK and that is where I learnt the elements of real research. Two very important elements make any research valid.

One is the exclusion of bias, which is tested by a double blind test during which neither the tester nor the researched subjects know the control and test items. The researched subjects may take a substance which maybe a real substance or a placebo. The research environment is highly controlled to ensure unbiased research. However, a researcher, working for a company, which produces the substance, could be biased. Alternatively, the research subjects may feel obliged to test with bias a free supply of fitness supplements.

Another important element , which ensures the validity of a research, is the sample's size and quality. To put it simply, a research project that only tests 10 people out of the billions of people on Earth is rubbish. Often, depending on a research, even a thousand subjects are not enough. The sample quality refers to the representativeness of a sample. If a researcher tests 1000 athletes for the effects of fast food on health and afterwards states that it is applicable to the general population, it is, yes, you guessed, rubbish!

Truth about Bodybuilding Supplements
Only for Professional Bodybuilders

I laugh when I see mega national companies claiming to deliver great results, but if you dig deeper, the sample was too small and not representative of their main customers, thus highly biased through and through.

There is one more trick of a few fitness companies. It is called a Proprietary Mix. Some bodybuilding supplements have a mixture of very expensive ingredients, thus companies try to undercut their competitors on price. How do they do it? It is simple: If a supplement contains 3 ingredients a company can claim that they have a more efficient mixture of these ingredients plus a fourth ingredient which is often cheap. They do not have to disclose the proportions because it is a proprietary mix, hence it is a secret. Be aware of the supplement company, which adds other ingredients and hides the amount of expensive ingredients in their supplement because you might be buying a supplement with a cheap ingredient at a premium price.

Now that you have a general understanding of how companies sell fitness supplements you can turn the situation around. Awareness saves you from being duped.

Truth about Bodybuilding Supplements

Only for Professional Bodybuilders

WELL KNOWN EXPENSIVE BRANDS VS UNKNOWN CHEAP BRANDS

It is paramount that the supplement you consume is of the highest quality. Every year many thousands of people die or fall ill because of toxic or low-grade supplements. Because bodybuilding powders, liquids and capsules are all artificial products, a stage in the manufacturing process can poison the supplement, thus it is poisonous for you. You might think you have bought a bargain priced Creatine (the most popular bodybuilding supplement) when, in fact, you have bought tainted Creatine because of its low grade. More importantly, it might be toxic due to the unregulated manufacturing processes, the companies cutting corners and the preservatives and fillers inside it.

I have to remain completely unbiased to be professional in my research on bodybuilding supplements. Thus, I cannot recommend to you any of the brands and, besides, the brands themselves vary from region to region. However, I recommend that you use products of only those companies, which have their laboratories and production lines in the countries with the strictest food and substance regulations. I am not familiar with the food and substance regulations of all the countries in the United Nations, but, using common sense and with a degree of certainty, I can write that a bodybuilding supplement from the Developed West can be more or less trusted as appropriate measures are taken by the Developed West to protect you from poisons. You will receive the real deal. Always find out the origin of the supplement and see that it does not contain chalk powder.

RECOMMENDED DOSAGES FOR BODYBUILDERS

This chapter is written to eliminate any confusion caused by supplement labels and the terms RDA and RDI on them. RDA stands for Recommended Daily Allowance or Recommended Dietary Allowance and RDI stands for Recommended Daily Intake. RDA was developed during the Second World War by a committee of the United States Academy of Sciences (later renamed Food and Nutrition Board) to determine the minimum nutrition requirement for army personnel. Later, the Food and Nutrition Board began to research the recommended daily intake for every nutrient known to man and for different population groups e.g. military or civilian. However, the Food and Nutrition Board did not research the dietary requirement of bodybuilders who are trying to increase their muscle mass. Their advice was always based on the average person, representative of the general population. As you might know, the general population is inactive and mostly sedentary. The recommendations were developed just to maintain your body and prevent you from becoming ill. They were not developed for gaining muscle mass and frequent, grueling workouts.

Athletes, bodybuilders and Olympians generally completely ignore the Recommended Daily Allowance and they often ignore the Recommended Daily Intake. It is just beyond common sense to compare an obese

sedentary person with someone who visits the gym at least four times a week and arrives there sweating due to a pre-gym grueling workout.

The RDI, Recommended Daily Intake, for protein averages around 0.8g per 1 kilogram of body weight (1 kilogram is approximately 2 lb). It is annoying to know that, so far, a reliable and authoritative study is not available to provide the RDI for physically active people.

RDA and RDI are based on the Body Mass Index proportion of the body weight to the height. The formula for BMI is:

$$BMI = \frac{weight\,(lb) \times 703}{height\,(in) \times height\,(in)} \quad \text{or} \quad BMI = \frac{weight\,(kg)}{height\,(m) \times height\,(m)}$$

BMI measurements are not designed for muscular people. BMI measurements ignore the lean muscle in a greatly developed bodybuilder's body. Muscle is 18% heavier than fat and a muscular person has significantly more muscle mass. According to the BMI guidelines, a muscular person is obese. A person with a BMI of 25 or over is considered obese. However, this does not apply to bodybuilders or athletic people. At the age of 34 in 1982 during the peak of his career as a muscular actor, Arnold Schwarzenegger had a BMI of 31, which is considered to be grossly obese. Of course, he was not obese but very muscular. This proves that BMI is just complete rubbish. A better measurement of your leanness is your body fat percentage and your waist measurement. Unbelievably, even the weight of your body is more or less irrelevant. Remember muscles are heavy and a well-built man has more muscle.

However, I have to be cautious. There is a more important term known as UL (tolerable Upper intake Levels) – taking a particular nutrient (supplement in our case) above, this level can be harmful. It stipulates the highest level of nutrients an average person can consume daily, based on the most recent scientific data. I would personally avoid exceeding this level. The UL (Upper Level) can be changed if future scientific data suggests a change. My recommendation is to stick to Western Block Supplement companies due to the comparatively stricter requirement for food safety, which is mostly up to date, in Western countries.

RESUME

If you are a hard working bodybuilder ignore RDI (Recommended Daily Intake) and RDA (Recommended Daily Allowance), instead make sure you do not exceed your UL (Tolerable Upper Intake Level).

For a hard working bodybuilder, BMI (Body Mass Index) is irrelevant. To measure your progress, use Body Fat and Waist Measurements and visually measure yourself in a mirror.

Truth about Bodybuilding Supplements
Only for Professional Bodybuilders

MUSCULAR BODY LAWS

Do not misunderstand me. I am in favor of fitness supplements, otherwise I would not have written this book. Supplements are like additives to preserve a car's engine and its other parts. The car still needs fuel and it needs good quality fuel so that the car can run smoothly. You can upgrade its engine and body but, without the correct fuel, it will not start and, without the right additives, it will break down quickly. Even worse, if you use additives incorrectly then there is a significant risk that it will break down very soon.

To achieve your bodybuilding goals, you have to follow three laws:

1.   Muscular Body Law 1 - You must have a healthy diet and lifestyle. If you do read many fitness magazines and watch muscular actors on TV, you must know that food and drink is the biggest factor of any bodybuilding success. We are programmed by the media and lifelong habits to eat what we eat and behave as we do. This book is for studying fitness supplements and the topic of a healthy lifestyle will be covered by another book, which I hope to publish in the future.

2.   Muscular Body Law 2 – Hard Gym Work. Eating healthily will help you gain a slender, attractive shape, but it will not build your muscles

unless part of your job or lifestyle involves muscle development. Again, you have to apply the correct bodybuilding routines e.g. you never see a muscular professional runner or cyclist. This is because they concentrate on developing so-called long twitch muscles instead of short twitch muscles. If a muscular physique is not your prime goal, then carrying out cardio workouts is preferable for you. Looking at exercising from all angles, if you want to become muscular, you need to exercise. Even those who inject steroids in themselves have to exercise to gain muscle. Muscles do not grow because of a magic potion. Again, this book is for studying fitness supplements and the topic of gym training will be covered another book which I hope to publish in the future as well.

3. Muscular Body Law 3 – Supplements. The supplements should be the correct supplements for your specific goals. They should be taken in the correct dosage, in the correct combination and at the correct time. Let me repeat myself, because it is important to reconfirm knowledge, if you have an unhealthy lifestyle without fitness workouts or with incorrect workouts, using supplements will not help you to become muscular. A good diet and workout are more effective than any supplement or drug on their own.

Because of our quick results mentality, we try to gain quick results by using a few magic potions without addressing the root cause first. It is like

fertilizing sand and planting a fir tree in it. Just think about your childhood movies and cartoons. In them, the good person consumes a magical substance and becomes a super hero. This "magic pill" attitude has been ingrained in us since our childhood.

Supplements will help you reach your goals faster if you have strong foundations as it is shown in the picture below.

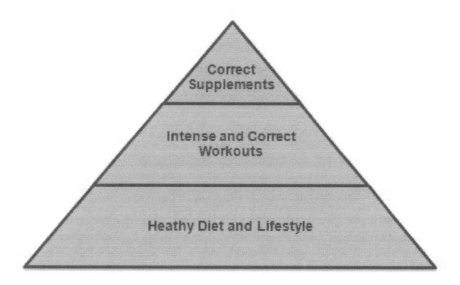

Now, as you know the main principles of becoming muscular, you are on the correct stage to learn about supplements: how they work, how to use them and when to use them.

RESUME

Muscular Body Laws:

1.   The base of the Muscular Body Pyramid is a Healthy Diet and Lifestyle

2.   The middle stage of the Muscular Body Pyramid is Intense and Correct Workouts

3.   The top stage of the Muscular Body pyramid is Correct Supplements

PROTEIN SUPPLEMENTS

Proteins are one of the three-macro nutrients. In this context, macro nutrients are the nutrients which we eat in large amounts. We primarily consume macronutrients to sustain life and produce energy. The two other macro nutrients are Fat and Carbohydrates. Protein is essential for building and repairing most of our lean body tissue, and for our bodies to make new cells and repair damaged cells. Our bodies can sometimes burn protein for energy e.g. when the diet is not balanced. Our muscles are made from protein, which constitutes around 75% of our muscle tissues.

Proteins vary from each other; hence, they each have different qualities as their structures differ from one protein to another. However, all of these structures consist of amino acids, which are the building blocks of proteins. Our bodies break down protein into amino acids for use by our bodies. There are twenty-two amino acids; nine are Essential for adults, twelve are Non-Essential for adults, humans do not use one amino acid, Pyrrolysine. Some Non-Essential amino acids are essential for infants and growing children or people with various illnesses. For example, Histidine was classified as Non-essential, but recent scientific studies have found that it becomes deficient in people over time.

Essential amino acids are essential not because they are more important than the others, but, because our body cannot synthesize them. The synthesis of protein is not possible without the presence of all nine amino acids, thus, to increase your muscle mass, you need all of the nine Essential amino acids.

Non-Essential amino acids can be produced by our bodies from other amino acids and molecules. Your body cannot operate efficiently without non-essential amino acids altogether because, depending on the type of stresses your body experiences, some of them become Essential as our body cannot produce enough of them. So they become Semi-Essential, also known as Conditionally Essential. However, there is a debate in the scientific community about which amino acid is Essential, Semi-Essential or Non-Essential.

I mentioned before that Non-Essential amino acids become Essential depending on the physical stresses we experience, hence these amino acids are called Semi-Essential. Bodybuilding physically stresses your body; it is a good and healthy stress, which is beneficial for your physical and mental being. For example, during a grueling and frequent bodybuilding program, Alanine becomes Semi-Essential and BCAAs (Branch Chained Amino Acids that are a mix of Leucine, Isoleucine and Valine) move from Essential to Highly Recommended during the workout.

For those expensive supplements to become value for money, the bodybuilding exercises must be really grueling and frequent.

Have a look at Glutamine to understand the conditionality of amino acids. Glutamine is the most abundant amino acid in your body and it is not needed as supplementation for those whose body fat percentage is in the double digits. If your body fat percentage is a single digit, your muscles will be compromised and burnt for energy when you work out intensely. However, if your body fat is above 10%, your body will not burn your muscles for energy, instead it will burn the food you ate that day and, your fat and glucose reserves. Of course, it is not an exact science. However, this demonstrates that Glutamine, the most abundant protein in your body, becomes essential when you work out hard. This only applies for those whose body fat is below 10% i.e. those who are skinny or already decently fit.

It is a highly debatable topic to determine which amino acids are actually essential when you workout, hence there are no hard and fast rules about it. When someone advises you on this matter always have a look at the results the adviser himself has achieved. If his body's physique is your desired goal, follow his advice. However, be cautious if he is completely truthful and, reveals the steroids he uses or his sponsorship from a supplement company.

Here is a table of categorized amino acids for a healthy person performing grueling bodybuilding workouts:

Essential	Semi-Essential	Non-Essential
Histidine	Alanine	Arginine
Isoleucine*		Asparagine
Leucine*		Aspartic acid
Lysine		Cysteine
Methionine		Glutamic acid
Phenylalanine		Glutamine**
Threonine		Glycine
Tryptophan		Proline
Valine*		Selenocysteine
		Serine
		Tyrosine

*Highly recommended during hard and frequent workouts

**Recommended after a hard workout for a slim or decently fit person with body fat below 10%

Truth about Bodybuilding Supplements

Only for Professional Bodybuilders

RESUME

Proteins are the building blocks of your muscles.

Proteins consist of amino acids, which are Essential, Semi-Essential and Non-essential, depending on your body's fitness and the intensity of your training.

It is sensible to prioritize and supply yourself with Essential and Semi-Essential amino acids to ensure muscle growth.

REASONS FOR SUPPLEMENTING WITH PROTEIN POWDERS

Let us consider the reasons for using protein powders:

- Convenience
- Timely delivery when most needed
- Easily digestible compared to meat sources of protein
- Vegetarians increase their Protein consumption

Convenience – You do not "cook" your protein shakes. Instead, you can put them into a shaker, shake them with water or milk and the job is done. Because of our busy lifestyles, this option saves us time to visit a gym, instead of cooking. It is also cheaper than cooking a high quality steak with side dishes. Besides, at the time of writing this book, it is uncommon to eat a steak in a gym's changing room after a workout. Imagine that scene in your mind!

Timely delivery when most needed – When do you most need protein if you are building your muscles? The most obvious answer is straight after or during an intensive workout to provide highly required protein for muscle repair and growth. After a workout, your muscles are stressed, so your body needs to repair them. While your body is repairing your muscles, your muscles will increase in muscle mass so that you can lift more next time. If you do not consume enough protein after or during an intensive workout,

your body depletes the instant energy sources in your body (e.g. glucose) and it switches into starvation mode by sending signals to accumulate fat and crave for fast foods. Consequently, your body's recovery is slower and it becomes over-trained. In this over-trained state, your body will not increase your muscle mass efficiently and you will not recover enough to train harder next time. However, if you are really well organized and maintain a regular, protein rich diet (5 or more times a day); most likely you do not need protein powders unless you train like an Olympian. There is one big exception for those who are naturally skinny. No matter what they try, they cannot increase their weight or muscle mass. They have to train hard, but they would definitely benefit from protein powders.

Easily digestible compared to meat sources of protein – When you consume natural protein from meats and not from powders your body needs energy to digest it. So if you consumed 40 grams of protein as a steak, around 30% of this steak will be used by your body to absorb the remaining protein. In other words, 12 grams out of 40 grams will be burnt to absorb the remaining 28 grams. It is a high ratio in comparison to Fats and Carbohydrates with 8% and 3% ratios, accordingly.

This fact is a double-edged sword. If you are trying to lose weight using a high protein diet, only eat natural proteins in the form of meats and avoid protein powders completely. They are pre-digested, thus you will consume most of the protein that will accumulate on your waist as fat.

Additionally, because real meat proteins induce a calorie burning effect, they also generally speed up your metabolism, thus burning more fat. Proteins are also known for their filling factor; the more protein there is in your diet the more likely you will feel that you ate enough with fewer calories in your food.

It must be mentioned that the advice on eating high quality and high protein content food from fitness magazines is fine. They compile delicious recipes. In fact, I have tried many of their recipes several times, but the cost of eating such high quality food was huge. For example, king prawns for breakfast, lobsters for snacks, freshly squeezed pomegranates for your antioxidant boost, accompanied by the most exclusive cuts of meat and fish, yes and don't forget my favorite black caviar on a toasted whole meal olive bread to give me enough omegas to produce testosterone. Hmm, where do I find a servant now to have it eight times a day anywhere I go? Right, I will need my servants to travel with me... I hope my sarcasm was obvious, so be realistic and develop solutions that are suitable for you.

If you train like a professional and want to bulk up as soon as possible while controlling your dietary calorie consumption, you will find a better

value for money in consuming protein powders because your body absorbs most of the protein in the powders to repair and build muscles, hence protein powders are more efficient and are generally cheaper per gram of protein converted into muscle mass.

However, do not over consume protein powders. You have teeth, k-nines and a meat digesting system for the digestion of solid foods. Your body needs solid food to function properly. Think back to when you may have had an upset stomach due to protein powders. It may have been a signal to eat more solid foods.

Some bodybuilders are vegetarians and often lack protein in their diets, so they supplement themselves with protein powders. In my opinion, vegetarianism is unhealthy because a vegetarian lacks those essential meat nutrients for health and energy. Even cows provide protein to their calves in the form of milk. Besides, if humans were similar to cows we would have longer digestive tracks because it takes longer for grass to be digested and absorbed than meats. Besides this point, the vegetarian debate is too large to be covered by this book. In short, modern health advice is against vegetarianism. In fact, a well-informed doctor (e.g. a surgeon) will advise that humans are not designed to be fully healthy on a vegetarian diet.

If you do not eat meat, eggs and milk, please consume at the very least vegetarian protein powders alternatives (e.g. whey protein powders) to develop your muscles. However, avoid soy protein as recent research into soy products suggests that it is very dangerous for your health. A study states that that soy destroys your thyroid gland. This destruction is a cause of tiredness and obesity. The same research claims that soy is very high in plant based estrogen, which leads to cancer, infertility and a low libido. However, because soy is in almost every food product and does have the property of mixing ingredients with water, you might want to consider a compromise in some instances. We will discuss soy in more detail in a later section about Soy Protein Powders.

RESUME

The main reasons for supplementing your diet with Protein Powders:

- Convenience
- Timely delivery when most needed
- Easily digestible compared to meat sources of protein
- Vegetarians increase their protein consumption

Proteins from real foods help you to lose more weight. They satisfy your hunger with a smaller amount and extra calories are burnt while digesting them.

Sometimes it is not realistic or economical to gain high amounts of high quality proteins from a diet.

Vegetarians will especially benefit from protein powders because their diets typically lack proteins. Vegetarians typically choose soy protein because it is not animal based, however, a few studies advise against consuming soy.

PROTEIN SUPPLEMENT VARIETIES

There are a few types of protein powder. Depending on your body and preferences, you can favor one over another. Additionally, protein supplements like protein shots and bars are also available. The supplement market is constantly advancing and more forms of protein supplements might be sold in the future. Below, I will discuss the types of protein supplements currently available on the market. I will discuss the differences between them. Here is a list of these types of protein supplements:

- Whey Protein Concentrate
- Whey Protein Isolate
- Micro Filtration (Ultra Filtration) Whey Protein
- Cross Flow Micro Filtration Whey Protein
- Hydrolyzed Whey Protein
- Egg Protein
- Casein Protein
- Soy Protein
- Pea, oats and other protein powders
- Blends
- Protein shots
- Protein bars

WHEY PROTEIN CONCENTRATE

Whey Protein Concentrate is the cheapest and most common protein supplement on the market. Whey Protein is a mixture of water-mixable proteins (globular proteins, as well as fibrous proteins which are insoluble e.g. meat) which are a liquid by-product of cheese. Whey Protein Concentrate has a small amount of Fat and Cholesterol. It also contains a low amount of Carbohydrates in the form of Lactose, which can cause health issues, if your stomach is ultra sensitive or you already consume plenty of Lactose from dairy products. From my personal experience, when my stomach could not digest whey proteins I switched to Egg Protein Powder even though Egg Protein Powder is considerably more expensive. The actual amount of protein you gain from Whey Protein Concentrate Powder Mixes is 30% to 80%. Read the labels to make sure you are buying real proteins and not fillers.

Whey Protein Concentrate is beneficial for muscle development, bone health, appetite regulation, the health of the bones and the immune system. An advantage of Whey Protein Concentrate is that it is digested slowly, thus it is a better option if you wish to supplement over night when your body is repairing itself. Whey Protein Powder is the most commonly consumed powder because most people gain positive results through it and it is one of the cheapest protein powders. Try it and if your stomach can digest it, then congratulations you will save more money in comparison to other powder proteins.

RESUME

Whey Protein Concentrate is the most popular and cheapest protein supplement; hence, its quality is not the best.

Because of its slow absorption rate, the best time to consume Whey Protein Concentrate is during the night.

Truth about Bodybuilding Supplements

Only for Professional Bodybuilders

WHEY PROTEIN ISOLATE

Whey Protein Isolate is of a higher quality than Whey Protein Concentrate. The difference is in their methods of production. Manufacturers filter milk protein so that Whey Protein Isolate virtually becomes Lactose, Carbohydrate, Fat and Cholesterol free. Whey Protein Isolate has a very high protein content – around 90% - so when you are calculating your price per gram of protein take this in to consideration. Different studies conducted by different protein manufacturers are claimed to have different absorption rates which vary from 30 minutes to over 3 hours.

Whey Protein Isolate is absorbed faster than Whey Protein Concentrate; hence, it is suitable for use during or after a hard workout session. Another great time to consume Whey Protein Isolate is in the morning to replenish your body's reserves, as you did not eat for many hours. Take Whey Protein Isolate in the morning if you want to maximize your efforts to increase your muscle mass.

Whey Protein Isolate is produced through different methods. Depending on the method, the Whey Protein Isolate will be of higher or lower quality. In this case, it is worth mentioning that lower quality Whey Protein Isolate is not bad or useless. The degree of quality reflects the concentration of protein in it.

The oldest production method of Whey Protein Isolate uses the characteristics of the protein molecules some of which are electro charged. A charged particle can be extracted by applying an electromagnetic field. It is similar to playing with magnets, which attract each other. It is called Filtering by Ion Exchange because electro charged particles contain ions. This method produces protein powders with 90% protein content. They are easier to digest, easy to mix and their prices are moderate. However, a disadvantage of the Ion Filtration method is that a few protein structures are destroyed in the process of applying electricity, thus these proteins are useless for the body. Another disadvantage is that the protein powders do not contain enough of some of the bioactive amino acids. This is because the process of ionization does not capture a few of the miniscule protein particles. These missed particles have many healthy, useful properties such as the capability to boost the immune system and combat viruses.

This is because the ion exchange process does not capture and retain the smaller biologically active Whey protein fractions. This is a notable disadvantage of ion exchange proteins since numerous studies demonstrate the important health benefits of active whey protein fractions such as Glycomacropeptides, Proteose peptone and Lactoferrin. FYI - Lactoferrin is also a potent booster for the immune system and it has strong antiviral properties.

RESUME

Whey Protein Isolate is considered a protein supplement with a high protein concentration and purity; however, the production process eliminates a few useful protein micro particles.

Whey Protein Isolate is digested within a 30 minute to 3 hours period, thus it is recommended to be consumed after or during a workout.

MICRO FILTRATION (ULTRA FILTRATION) WHEY PROTEIN

Micro filtration (Ultra filtration) is a process which uses filtering membranes to screen out Fat and Lactose, resulting in a whey product containing up to 85% protein and as little as 1 percent fat. Micro Filtration Whey Protein is considered to a protein supplement with a high absorption rate. This protein powder is absorbed within 30 minutes and 3 hours.

The primary disadvantage of Filtered Whey Protein as opposed to the ion-exchange variety is that the filtered types are not completely pure. True, Ion-Exchange Protein can contain 90% pure protein and Filtered Whey Protein Isolate contains 85% to 87% protein on average.

Filtered Whey Protein also contains slightly higher amounts of Fat and Lactose, although the differences are not significant for the average consumer. Filtered Whey Proteins also have advantages however. They have higher levels of valuable whey protein fractions such as Glycomacropeptides, Proteose Peptone and Lactoferrin.

RESUME

Micro Filtration Whey Protein is absorbed quickly; hence, it is best to take it during or after a workout

Micro Filtration Whey Protein contains more essential and useful micro protein particles in comparison to Whey Protein Isolate.

CROSS FLOW MICRO FILTRATION WHEY PROTEIN

The Cross Flow Micro Filtration method was developed to solve some of the denaturing problems that were caused by the ion exchange method. It is similar to the micro filtration process.

The process is used to make proteins highly soluble and retain a higher level of calcium. It yields a good proportion of BCAA's and is an excellent source of fuel. Avonmore-Waterford patents this process, so there is an added cost for the product, but if it is within your budget, it is worth the extra cost.

The Cross Flow Micro Filtration process produces an isolate that has greater than 90% protein with no Fat or Lactose. Unlike the ion exchange process, Cross Flow Micro Filtration leaves almost 100% of the protein and the important peptides intact.

Bodybuilders also prefer Cross Flow Micro Filtration Whey Protein because they believe that it is a Golden Middle between Whey Protein Concentrate and Hydrolyzed Whey Protein. They argue Hydrolyzed Protein is too pre-digested, broken-up and hence unstable, however, an actual comprehensive study has not proved or disapproved this. In any case, I will discuss Hydrolyzed Whey Protein next.

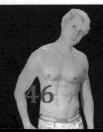

Truth about Bodybuilding Supplements
Only for Professional Bodybuilders

RESUME

Cross Flow Micro Filtration Whey Protein is the best and fastest absorbed protein supplement, but it is also one of the most expensive. It is as pure as Whey Protein Isolate as it contains essential micro protein particles.

Cross Flow Micro Filtration Whey Protein is considered the Golden Middle for fast-absorbed protein powders because it is not completely denatured for fast absorption in comparison to Hydrolyzed Proteins. If a protein is too denatured, it breaks down before being digested by the body.

The best time to take Cross Flow Micro Filtration Whey Protein is during or after a workout.

HYDROLYZED WHEY PROTEIN

Hydrolyzed powder is broken down further than any other whey protein. This is so that your body will absorb protein faster, thus this powder is highly recommended for consumption during and immediately after a workout. The absorption time is between 20 minutes and 1.5 hours.

The beauty of Hydrolyzed Proteins is that they are absorbed in half the time of any other protein currently available at the time of writing this book. There is another advantage of it – some people argue that when hydrolyzed proteins are absorbed the body needs less energy to digest it, thus less calories and fat are burnt. In other words, the thermal effect is decreased, but those people are missing a point. When sportsmen take the proteins their intention is to deliver protein to their muscles in the most effective way, not to increase their thermal fat burning rate.

I would recommend using Hydrolyzed Protein with caution only after you have tried other proteins, which you have compared. The reason for this caution is that the whole heat-treatment and pre-digestion methods might destroy some proteins and their components; hence, they become unusable for our bodies.

There were some reports that claimed it might cause diarrhea and self-proclaimed experts online suppose that this is caused by the user's bad stomach. This is a rare occurrence. I disagree with them because Hydrolyzed Protein Powder gave me diarrhea. To conduct my own research, I requested my doctor to test me and I was fine. My solution is to try various brands until a suitable brand is discovered. In my case, it was Egg Protein Powder.

Another possible reason for diarrhea is a particular process, which is used to produce the powder. The solution to this is to switch to a different brand, but if all the available companies use this particular process you will have to switch to a different type of protein.

Hydrolyzed Protein Powder is one of the most expensive types of Whey Protein. Possibly, you cannot find a better protein powder for pre, during and post workout. It is more expensive because it is produced through more processes.

However, if you are a person who likes to have the best of the best, but this powder causes diarrhea then reconsider your options. If you have diarrhea, your body cannot absorb the Hydrolyzed Protein Powder, thus your body gets rid of it. My point is that you should not buy the most prestigious product; instead, you should find the one, which is suitable for you.

RESUME

Hydrolyzed Whey Protein Powder is the most expensive protein powder because more manufacturing processes are employed to break down proteins into the smallest possible size for super fast absorption. The absorption time is believed to be between 20 minutes and 1.5 hours.

Many will argue that it is too fine and unstable after the break down and, thus, by the time it reaches the stomach, it is useless as it is denatured.

If you have diarrhea because of consuming Hydrolyzed Whey Protein Powder, then switch to less denatured Protein Powders.

Hydrolyzed Whey Protein Powder is highly recommended and preferable to other powders for during and immediately after workouts.

EGG PROTEIN

There are a few types of Egg Protein on the market. Some of the powders are enhanced for better mixability and quicker absorption and some are just plain egg white powder. Plain egg white powder does not appeal to me because you can eat boiled egg whites and save money while eating one of the most perfect protein sources. My own preference is Enhanced Egg Protein Powder because its manufacturing processes are more sophisticated and less crude than simple egg white powder. Depending on the quality of the manufacturing process, it is absorbed faster and more effectively.

Another option to consider is a relatively new Egg Protein Powder with a fertilized egg yolk. This type of fertilized yolk has been proven to stop the blockers, which prevent muscle development. To find out if your egg protein powder has it read the ingredients. The ingredients will contain fertilized egg. Yes, it does increase the price as well.

Enhanced Egg Protein Powder is by far my favorite protein source. Think about it, Whey Protein is a by-product of milk and cheese production, thus the sources of it are relatively cheaper than egg proteins. Eggs can be a very expensive form of protein in the form of protein powders. The next most expensive is chicken and then lamb and fish proteins.

Egg proteins are considered perfect because eggs contain every essential amino acid and branch chain amino acid, as well as Glutamic acid. It has the highest amount of Alanine, which is very useful for recovery after a workout.

Egg protein has the highest Protein Efficiency Ratio, thus more protein is used by your body to increase your muscle mass. Some people prefer Whey Protein Isolate because the proportional amount of BCAAs in it is higher than in Egg Protein. BCAAs are directly metabolized in muscles without the involvement of the liver. Yes, it is right, but if you want to add more BCAAs pre, post or during a hard workout then you might as well supplement BCAAs separately rather than depend on powders. Nevertheless, the recommended amounts for BCAAs pre, post and during a workout are too high to be covered sufficiently by protein powders. Please read the recommendations for BCAAs later in this book.

The absorption rate of Egg Protein Powder is quite high at 1.5 and 3 hours, so it is a great protein powder for during and post workouts.

Ball State University conducted an experiment in which a few out of 17 over trained men, who trained for 4 weeks, took Egg Protein Powder, while the rest took a placebo powder. Because of Egg Protein's richness, absorbability and bioavailability, just 0.88 grams of Egg Protein per pound

of body weight (or kg) was enough to prevent overtraining. Their testosterone also increased. We all know that testosterone is crucial for increasing muscle mass.

One thing is certain. Because Egg Protein does not contain Lactose and it is manufactured with a minimal amount of processes possible, it is the safest way to consume protein powders. I performed a mini-online research and, at the time of writing this book, I did not discover any complaints of diarrhea. However, some reports state that it causes bloating and gas in some users. If you notice it within yourself, switch to another protein powder.

RESUME

Enhanced Egg Protein Powders are the most complete source of proteins for a bodybuilder. Because of its quality, most of the proteins are absorbed and not denatured which leads to fewer stomach problems.

Plain Egg White Powders are not as effective as Enhanced Egg Protein Powders due to their crude production processes.

Enhanced Egg Protein Powders with Fertilized Yolk stop blockers, which prevent muscle development.

The absorption rate for Enhanced Egg Protein Powder is between 1.5 and 3 hours. This is perfect as a post workout supplement.

CASEIN PROTEIN

Casein Protein Powder is also known as milk protein. 80% of all milk proteins are Whey Protein and the remaining 20% is Casein Proteins. What differentiates Casein Protein Powder from other proteins is its slow absorption rate – Casein Protein is absorbed within 7 hours – Casein Protein Powder has the slowest absorption rate on the market, thus it is very suitable for consumption at night. Most of the recovery and muscle development processes happen while we are asleep. This is why many bodybuilders think Casein is the best for them. Casein Protein Powder is definitely not a pre or post workout protein supplement.

Some preclinical studies on rodents observed the extra anti-inflammatory and anti-cancer properties of Casein Protein. Currently, these results are being tested on humans.

However, the efficiency rate of Casein Protein Powder is one of the lowest amongst the protein powders. It is only 2.5 compared to 3.8 of Egg Protein Powder which is 34% more efficient, or another Night Recovery Protein – Whey Concentrate has an efficiency ratio of 3.2 which makes it 22% more efficient. Casein Protein Powder also has an incomplete amount of all the types of amino acids – building blocks that the body extracts from proteins.

Even stating all of the above, the use of Casein Protein Powder can be attractive because of a Slow Digestion Concept. This is similar to Low GI diets.

GI is an abbreviation for the Glycemic Index of carbohydrate food. At a higher index, the food is absorbed quicker. If the produced amount of energy from the food is higher than the amount of calories consumed e.g. lying on a sofa or swimming in a lake, then the difference in energy will be stored as fat. On the other hand, if the amount of energy per hour is more than the amount of food burnt as energy per hour then you will burn fat. Therefore, if you eat white bread, which has High GI, then the whole amount of energy will be burnt in less than an hour. A word of warning, you better be physically active enough to prevent forming fat above your six-pack. On the other hand, if you eat the same amount of food energy in the form of whole meal bread with Low GI then the food energy will be burnt over 3 hours instead of 1 hour. This gives your body more time to burn food without converting it into fat and it relieves you body system of sudden spike stresses.

In the case of Casein Powders, you cannot use GI directly because GI is for Carbohydrates, not proteins. However, the same principle applies if you consume your protein regularly in reasonable amounts over a longer period, then you will avoid the excess energy from the conversion of protein

into fat on your six-pack, hence you will avoid wasting protein. However, Casein Protein is low in its efficiency ratio of protein absorption, hence it is more wasteful. Now you know that Casein Protein has two contradictory factors, thus you will have to strike a balance, depending on your life style, expense and tolerance of your body to different protein powders. If you have diarrhea after consuming a certain type of protein powder, your body is not tolerant of a particular supplement or vice versa. Casein Protein Powder is suitable for those people who have a very strict diet.

Another great quality of Casein Protein Powder is that it is produced from milk, hence it contains plenty of Calcium – high calcium intake aids fat elimination. A study conducted by the International Journal of Obesity found that those who consume high amounts of Calcium show increased fecal fat and energy use which leads to a slimmer you.

Another study in Boston researched fat loss and lean muscle gain amongst those who take Casein Protein or Whey Protein during a period of dieting and resistance training. They found that those who consumed Casein Protein burnt more fat and gained more strength in their chests, shoulders and legs. This is a very interesting result, because people who burn fat, lose some muscle tissue as the body eats into the tissues when slimming down. This and all of the above indicate that Casein Protein Powder is designed for those who diet to lose fat whilst exercising. Casein Powder will not prevent some loss of muscle during slimming, but it will ensure a minimal loss of muscle.

RESUME

Casein Powder is also perfect for those who try to lose fat as Casein is slowly digested which uses extra energy.

Casein Powder has many other health benefits such as anti-inflammatory properties and high calcium content which aids further fat loss.

Casein Protein Powder is the least efficient in transporting protein to your muscle cells.

Although it is the least efficient, it does provide proteins over a long period, for example, during a sleep of over 7 hours. This is unique to this product. Most muscle recovery happens over night. Because of Casein's extremely slow absorption rate, it is perfect for overnight supplementation. It is definitely not a post workout supplement.

SOY PROTEIN

Soy Protein Powders are available in different forms like Whey Protein as Concentrate, Isolate and Predigested etc. The soy proteins themselves are extracted from soya beans immersed in a watery solution. However, there is a reason why some manufacturers add it into a protein blend, it is cheap and promoted by the entire global soy industry, but often if it is cheap it is rubbish.

Most modern news media organizations seemed to be promoting soy at the time of writing this book. Let me state straight away without further ado; my views are based on my research and experience. Avoid soy products including Soy Protein Powders. Yes, it is extremely difficult to know the truth when there are so many strong opponents debating soy, and uncompleted studies on humans. It is better to be safe than sorry.

However, why do modern news media organizations promote soy products? Well to start, let us look at some of the pillars of the news media's operation. Modern media is in the business of selling news and its influence on you and me, unfortunately, is not the same as the influence of unbiased, intelligent, correct and scientific news. The modern news media follows popular fads to reach out to the most pockets and eyeballs. Twenty years ago, it was all about Global Freezing, now it is all about Global

Warming. Unfortunately, most of the information out there cannot be trusted to make the right choice. The news media is mostly about politics and, unfortunately, politics are not facts, but, sometimes, it is a bazaar of opinionated people pushing their own interests to attempt to "manage" or manipulate people to a particular end even if it is against the voters. It does not help that news must be primarily paid for by advertisers who want to sell their products. The whole discussion on the benefits of soy is helped by theories, which state that if we all somehow become cows and do not eat meat, we will solve the hunger problems of the world. I repeat myself again if we were like cows, we would have a longer digestive track and this is, a proven, biological, scientific fact.

Reputable scientific studies have been made on various animals; the results were mind-boggling, thus why is it not acted upon by the regulators? Maybe this is because the industry is too huge? Official studies have not been made on humans and scientists will need a human life-long data to realize the full effects of soy on humans. This situation is similar to when tobacco companies were denying that smoking causes cancer because it was not proved in humans yet.

Many of the supposed health harms and benefits are associated with soy Isoflavones, plant compounds that mimic human estrogen. These compounds have been found to cause infertility and pre-mature puberty. These compounds have also been found to disrupt the development of children. Soy has been known to prevent the absorption of various vitamins and minerals and, develop breasts in men. Soy has been found to badly affect the Thyroid Gland, which is essential for your energy levels and keeping you slim. Moreover, most relevant for bodybuilding, soy is known to block protein absorption and lower testosterone levels in some people. Are these findings enough to convince you to avoid the consumption of soy?

Some might say, what about the Chinese who lived on soy for a millennia? The Chinese began to eat soya beans around 2500 years ago after they learnt how to ferment it to neutralize its harmful toxins; somehow, even they knew soy is not that great. In traditional Chinese diets, soy is used in small amounts as a condiment to meat. Around 2000 year ago, soy products were used in Chinese monasteries to promote abstinence, thus reducing testosterone. It is only recently that soy is eaten in large amounts, unfermented and highly processed. Let me finish this chapter by highlighting that, considering all the commotion around soy and its incomplete research, the main principle here is: "Better be safe than sorry".

Regarding the above, we must realize that soy is almost in everything and we have to be very careful not to consume it. This is because soy products have preservative qualities and mix unmixable powders with water e.g. BCAA powder is notoriously near impossible to mix with water; however, a small addition of Soy Lecithin makes it mixable. A compromise can be made. If soy is not one of the main ingredients, it may be consumed.

RESUME

A preliminary research indicates that Soy Protein is bad for your health and bodybuilding goals. In the debate on soy, too much politics and interests are involved to discern the truth – better be safe than sorry and avoid soy.

Soy in Chinese cooking is fermented which is not harmful, but global industries are using unfermented soy because it is cheap.

PROTEIN BLENDS

There are numerous varieties of protein blends that claim to have fast absorbed proteins and slow absorbed proteins to meet both of your needs such as taking protein after a workout and supplementing protein after a workout period.

You have to be careful and avoid being conned because often companies just reduce the amounts of expensive protein types and increase the amounts of cheap proteins in their supplements and still charge premium price for them. Sometimes, they even add the cheapest, evil and unfermented soy protein.

Therefore, do read labels and find out if the mix is genuinely designed to combine the benefits of proteins and not to shove something cheap under your nose. My position on this is that protein powders of the correct types taken at the correct time for the correct purposes are more effective otherwise you just consume expensive supplements just to increase your stomach fat. It is easier to control your efforts with single purpose proteins. However, sometime there are circumstances when it is just convenient and economically more effective then it is justifiable to consume protein blends. In any case, the effectiveness depends on the type of blend and its promised benefits. It is similar to vitamins. Many vitamin supplements are

more effective when taken as a single supplement or in combination with an element that helps to absorb it. However, some vitamins and minerals negatively affect the absorption of their fellow vitamins and minerals. Ideally, if you want to supplement yourself, you have to take separate mixes at separate times for better absorption, but it is not convenient and very difficult to explain, so most people take one pill only. This is the current situation of the market and the companies are not entirely guilty. The same applies to protein blends, they are convenient and sometimes it is better to take them without too much concern.

One thing is for sure, as you are now knowledgeable about various protein powders and how they vary depending on the purpose of bodybuilding, you can choose the protein mix, which is suitable for you.

RESUME

Protein blends are numerous in their qualities and effects, however, you can apply the knowledge you gained in this book as any protein blend consists of separate protein powders as discussed in this book.

PROTEIN BARS AND SHOTS

Most of the protein bars and protein shots contain Hydrolyzed Whey, which is abundant in l-Glutamine, and BCAAs. One very important note here is that, to retain their quality, protein shots and bars should be kept in a fridge just like normal food.

Protein bars come in many varieties and price ranges. Often, cheap protein bars from a large supermarket chain contain ingredients you would never consume and they are not that nice to eat. Hence, you might as well buy protein powders if you want to save a little bit on price. There is no need to buy "cheap premium" protein bars if the taste is bad and the ingredients are rubbish or even toxic because big supermarket chains tend to use low quality ingredients, so what is the point? You might as well buy a protein powder which probably will be better for you.

Another type of protein bars are the delicious ones, packed with plenty of expensive proteins and high amounts of protein, around 30 grams or more of protein per bar. Because the price of these proteins bars is at a premium, it seems obvious that big supermarket chains can afford to put quality items into them. Still, you should be careful if you do not know the ingredients. They are trying to sell you water for gold, thus you have to be knowledgeable to get high quality protein bars when you pay top prices.

Many times, I have seen expensive products filled with inferior quality ingredients.

At any time, give me a delicious white chocolate strawberry bar with over 40 grams of protein. Give me that protein bar instead of a banana and a shake after a hard workout or as meal replacement when I prepare myself for a photo shoot. The price though is premium and, yes, it all comes down to your preferences and how much you want to spend. However, at any other time, a banana with a protein shake is a healthier option after a strenuous workout because it has less sugar and a safer impact on your Insulin levels. Safe insulin levels lower the chances of Type 2 Diabetes.

Protein shots come in colorful tubes. They are mostly Hydrolyzed Protein or even Predigested. It is very important to keep them refrigerated to prevent the protein from breaking down. If your wallet is thick, I definitely recommend protein shots as your preference for immediately after a workout.

RESUME

Protein shots and bars are best for during or after a workout because of their high sugar content. Sugar is good only after a strenuous workout.

Decide on the quality of protein shots and bars by looking at types of protein powders they consist of. Protein shots and bars are mainly premium products, however, watch out for some made from cheap ingredients and sold expensively.

PEA, OATS AND OTHER PROTEIN POWDERS

Sometimes companies create new forms of protein, developed from almost anything. However, they are problematic because not enough research was conducted. Supplements need to be tested on animals for years and then for decades on humans. Separate and independent research teams must perform these tests.

Now you know the differences between Concentrated, Isolate, Micro filtered, Hydrolyzed proteins etc. the same applies to all types of protein powders. New proteins come on the market as we search for miracles. It is not possible to take a position on these new types of protein. Think about soy protein! When it came out it was a miracle protein for everyone but then, as studies followed, we found out that we should avoid it altogether.

You might speculate and say that it is better for a vegetarian to take Oat Protein Powder instead of Soy Powder, but this is just speculation and an unproven theory. This book is about the supplements that have accumulated enough research and have been tested and worked. Let us leave speculation to someone else.

RESUME

There are plenty of new protein powders; however, not enough research has been conducted into them, so only pure speculation remains.

Truth about Bodybuilding Supplements

Only for Professional Bodybuilders

VALUE FOR MONEY

I recommend to shop by price per gram of protein to see a true picture. Divide the price per tablet of the powder by the grams of proteins in the whole tablet. You will need to use your math skills to convert protein grams per 100 grams of powder into protein grams per tablet. Some supplement companies put the composition of the proteins in a tablet on the labels and separate them into protein components – amino acids. In my experience, this is an indication of a good quality supplement because it is stated from their research where as unscrupulous companies will not reveal all of their components because they just unsure of their own ingredients. However, a few persistent, unscrupulous companies might use this labeling method as a trick, so be aware.

Another important point is to understand is the Protein Efficiency Ratio. The higher the ratio, the more protein will be actually used by your muscles. Here are some values:

P.E.R's. (Protein Efficiency Ratios)
Egg protein: 3.8
Whey protein: 3.2
Beef protein: 2.9
Casein: 2.5
Soy protein concentrate: 2.2

As you can see egg protein is expensive, but it is 42% more efficient than, let us say, soy protein or 16% more efficient than whey protein, so if it is only 10% more expensive per gram of protein then chose egg protein. Besides, it is not only a better deal, but egg protein is more complete in its components and its manufacturing processes are fewer. I do not recommend soy protein in any case. To understand why, please read the chapter on soy protein.

Let us consider a hypothetical example; in this example we need a night protein, which is Whey Protein Concentrate, for recovery during our sleep. Another night protein, Casein, is at the same price, but, because it is less efficient than Whey Concentrate, we chose Whey Concentrate. Let us say, we decide to shop online and search specifically for Whey Protein Concentrate. We find some of the cheapest ones which we are now comparing. By the way, once you decide on two or three online shops search the internet for discount codes etc. for these shops and then take the promotions you find into consideration. Here, we have a Whey Protein Concentrate tablet label:

800 grams for $39

Serving size:	34 grams scoop	Per 100 grams
Energy	136 kcal / 573 kj	401 kcal / 1685 kj
Protein	22.1 grams	65 grams
Carbohydrates	4.5 grams	13.2 grams
Of which sugars (Lactose)	1.7 grams	5.1 grams
Fat	3 grams	9 grams
Of which MCTs	0.8 grams	2.5 grams
Dietary Fibre	1.1 grams	3.3 grams
Sodium	60 mg	175 mg
Lactase	34 mg	100 mg
All the Amino Acids detailed ...	...	...
...	...	...

There are 65 grams of protein in each 100 grams of the powder. In other words, 65% of the powder is protein, hence 800 grams of powder in a tablet, multiplied by 65% gives us 520 grams. The price is $39 so if we divide $39 by 520 grams it gives us 7.5 US Cents per gram of protein. Now, we can compare this with other supplements to pick the best supplement. Of course, you might not want to make any complicated calculations, but still you can use your own judgment and approximations.

But are we finished? Not yet, because it is a milk product, which has Lactose. It is present for 5.1 grams, which is 5.1%. This is just in the normal range of 2% to 8% of ordinary milk. In addition note that Lactase is included. (Do not confuse with Lactose). This is an enzyme to aid the digestion of Lactose and hence it helped you to avoid an upset stomach. Lactase is present in people who are genetically used to drinking milk as adults and there are different degrees of it. You see, the company put all the necessary ingredients in the supplement to deliver a great product.

Let us see further, it has an interesting Fat of MCTs. What are they? After a little bit of research, I found out they are Medium Chain Triglycerides – human produced fats. Because of one their relevant qualities, they are sometimes used to treat diarrhea which can be an absorption disorder. Just to let you know, you do need to absorb all the protein, which you consume.

Okay, so we also find out that the company produced its product in stringent West European laboratories. This assures us that it is pure and not toxic. It also details all of the product's ingredients.

It appears that this protein shake has many positive points. Well yes, it has 7.5 US Cents per gram of protein, thus another cheaper per gram of protein product should be considerably cheaper or a little cheaper but as reputable. However, no matter how cheap it is, if it is not produced in a reputable, quality controlled laboratory in a reputable country, then I recommend that you avoid it at all costs. You might be wasting your money on dummies, but, most sadly, you might be literately killing yourself because of impurities and poisons due to the lack of quality, appropriate production control, researched, and backed knowledge.

RESUME

While choosing a suitable protein powder you should rely on price per gram, efficiency of the type of the protein and its quality.

PROTEIN ABSORPTION

Be careful when you decide to increase the intake of protein overall. I only recommend consuming fast absorbing protein powders immediately after a hard workout. Slow absorbing proteins are more suitable when you are just increasing your protein intake. If your body absorbs proteins in under one hour and your protein calorie intake is higher than the calories you burn per hour and for repair immediately after a workout, then you will add excess calories as fat on your hips. Calories are calories, just because they come from proteins, that does not make them less dangerous.

Some argue that you will worry less if your plan is to bulk up without limitations and to become a little overweight to gain more muscles with a plan to lose weight later. In my experience, those who used the above-mentioned approach have never actually lost any fat later. Yes, some did become bigger, but I am after a cut physique with a clear six-pack and every muscle visible. After years of exercise in gyms and reading multiple bodybuilder biographies, I have not yet witnessed someone achieving that cut physique through the above-mentioned approach. If you are one of the elusive types who just cannot increase their weight, no matter how much you eat, then experiment with consuming quickly absorbed protein. It might work in consideration of your circumstance.

RESUME

If you are dieting to lose fat, use fast absorbent proteins only for pre, during or after workouts or in the morning. Additionally, use slow digesting protein supplements to increase your protein intake at any other time.

PROTEIN DOSAGES

Bodybuilding magazines and bodybuilders who are sponsored by supplement companies advise the excessive consumption of protein powders. There is a conflict of interests, which makes bodybuilding magazines unreliable in this matter. Supplement companies own many fitness magazines and even if a fitness magazine is not owned by a supplement company that magazine still depends on advertising revenue from supplement companies.

Earlier in the book, we discussed how often the research of supplement companies is not valid. The goal of these companies is to make more and more sales, thus they will find any possible way to make sales because the law does not always protect from ignorance and fallibility. These supplement companies would like you to believe that if you do not consume their protein shakes, then you will inevitably lose your muscles and this is complete rubbish. They portray their shakes to be essential for any bodybuilder and this is false. If you prefer protein shakes to real food it is your preference. Yes, it is convenient and is digested quicker by your body. However, if you prefer real food and sacrifice it for the sake of protein shakes, then think again; look at the food labels of good quality sausages, investigate how much protein is in delicious steaks, chickens, eggs or fishes. You will find that you can gain more protein from real food. Of

course, it is not as convenient and easy to cook healthy food in comparison to mixing a protein shake, so you will have to find a balance of your own in this matter.

Be very careful from someone you admire who promotes high protein diets with plenty of protein shakes of a particular brand. There is no reason to lose trust in your heroes. Eventually, they did become as fit as you would like to be but they probably did not reach this through protein shakes. They just want money like everyone, so they endorsed the products of supplement companies. If you do want to use protein shakes, your heroes will hopefully direct you to quality shakes, thus you will avoid poison and wasting money.

While deciding on your minimum intake of protein you have to consider the level of your activity. It was reported in many news media outlets that Michael Phelps, an outstanding American Olympic swimmer with a stunning athletic figure, consumed 12,000 calories a day during his period of intensive training and exhaustive competitions. This is the amount of calories some of us would like to eat over the whole week while visiting a gym a few times. This scenario also applies to your intake of protein; you need to consume extra protein only during a period of grueling bodybuilding. If you over eat protein, then, in one way or another, you body's fat will increase.

Therefore, what is the answer? How much protein should we consume to develop our muscles? The answer depends on the intensity and frequency of your bodybuilding regime. You can start by taking 2 to 3 grams of protein per kilogram of your body weight (1 to 1.5 grams per a pound of your body weight). Depending on your rate of recovery, and adjusting the portion accordingly. Also, remember that to effectively synthesize proteins, they must be supplemented with Carbohydrates. The weight of our bones, our water percentages, fat percentages, level of fitness, speed of metabolism are all different and vary, it is all a process of trial and error. We have to experiment with our own bodies.

RESUME

The advice of fitness magazines is not always reliable because they depend on advertisements of protein powders and supplements.
It is better to gain proteins from your diet rather than supplementing with them.

If you workout hard in the gym, then the dosage of 2 to 3 grams of protein per kilogram of your body weight (1 to 1.5 grams per a pound) is suitable.

We all have different bodies; hence, our optimal protein consumption will vary.

IMPORTANCE OF CARBOHYDRATES

If you surf online, you will find some utter nonsense that states proteins cannot be absorbed without Carbohydrates. Protein is a nutrient on its own and a human can survive on it. No matter which nutrients, such as Proteins, Carbohydrates or Fats, you take as fuel for your body, eventually, some part of them will be converted into Glucose. Glucose is essential for your body just as petrol is essential for a car. And, yes, your body can survive on one nutrient only. Note: I said survive, not prosper.

However, let us not jump from one extreme to another. Yes, you do need Carbohydrates to effectively use proteins. If you consume an excessive amount of protein, your digestive system slows down, thus the absorption of protein into your bloodstream through your stomach is slowed down. This also reduces the absorption of other nutrients such as vitamins, minerals and fluids. Every nutrient is essential if you subject your body to huge physical stresses during your bodybuilding venture. Intensive exercise does deplete many essential and various substances in your body. You must work out hard and smart to gain any serious bodybuilding results, be it a prominent six-pack or defined and huge biceps or that inverted, mesmerizing triangular back muscles to keep everyone's attention on the beach. My recommendation is to take at least twice as many Carbohydrates as Proteins.

RESUME

Although Carbohydrates are not essential for Protein absorption they are definitely recommended for overall effectiveness.

Take at least twice as many Carbohydrates as Proteins.

CREATINE

Creatine is one of the most popular fitness supplements and almost everyone has either heard about it or most likely used it with differing results. Understanding Creatine will also uncover a few mysteries of how other supplements work. For these reasons, I will cover Creatine in detail.

Creatine is a combination of three amino acids: Arginine, Glycine and Methionine. Creatine is naturally present in any meat, however, you would have to eat at least 5 decent sized steaks a day to consume enough Creatine to enhance your bodybuilding experience which would make you fat. Creatine is great as a supplement because your body cannot get enough of it to boost your efforts in the gym and you do not gain all those extra calories from Creatine supplement.

Creatine was first used by a British Olympic team during the 1992 Spanish Summer Olympics. Initially it caused fury as the British and Swiss lab results came out only after the Olympics and Creatine was used by the British team during the Olympics. This scandal spread the popular use of Creatine like a wildfire across the world. By the next Summer Olympics, which took place in the United States, around 80% of the Olympians were using it. Creatine's reputation was further enhanced in the United States through a doping scandal in 1998 when Mark McGwire broke a 37 years

long record on the Major League home run. Later, McGwire admitted to using Creatine, which is a combination of three amino acids together with Androstenedione, which is a pro-hormonal steroid. The link was created in the minds of the public, thus Creatine gained a similar image to a steroid. Of course, this is not true. Nonetheless, it sufficiently boosted the sales of Creatine. After the collapse of the Soviet Union, a few secret documents were discovered. They revealed that the Soviet Union used Creatine as far back as the 1970s. However, let me repeat: Creatine is not a steroid. It is a combination of Glycine, Arginine, and Methionine amino acids. In simple words, Creatine is a protein.

The downside of the Creatine hype is that its manufacturers are not interested in revealing any of its negative side effects, and they are not obliged to do this. You might be surprised, but it is a fact. This is because Creatine is a dietary supplement and not a drug, thus manufacturers can also produce Creatine of low quality and not be a subject to stringent control. This applies to most supplements in this book. However, due to lighter control, some brands of Creatine contain toxic substances. In addition, some manufacturers falsify a sense of innovation by not revealing all the ingredients and advertising it as a secret innovative formula.

CREATINE AT WORK

To develop your muscles, you need energy. We gain that energy from food. The consumed food is transformed into the energy, which you need to pump iron. Some food we eat is transformed into chemical energy in a form of Adenosine Tri Phosphate (ATP). When energy is needed for your muscles, ATP is broken down to create biological energy. This implies that the more muscle cells you have to store energy, the more instant lifting power you have. ATP in muscles is specifically created for short explosions of energy. Creatine regenerates ATP during intensive workouts. Before this, Creatine has to be converted into Phosphocreatine. To help this transformation, a few other ingredients should be taken for absorption. This is why some Creatine supplements contain Phosphate Creatine that is also known as Phosphagen.

Once ATP is broken down and energy is released it becomes Adenosine Di Phosphate (ADP). Normally, while we are not exercising strenuously ADP is retransformed into ATP using glucose stored in our bodies, but this process is very slow and inefficient while we are exercising. Instead there is another faster energy producing body process using Creatine only, Creatine is converted into Phosphate Creatine, which is transferred to our muscles to convert ADP. It releases the phosphate to transform ADP. The phosphate is retransformed into ATP for instant energy use. Do we need

that Creatine? On average, we use a pound (half a kilogram) of ATP during a strenuous workout. When, after a strenuous workout, ATP is not used, it is used to reconvert Creatine in to Phosphate Creatine.

CREATINE'S FIGHT AGAINST THE ACIDIC ENVIRONMENT OF THE MUSCLES

Lactic acid creates an acidic environment and decreases the pH balance of muscles making energy production less effective. Many argue that it is H+ ions that really tire muscles, not lactic acid, as such; however, it is all correlated and it is similar to deciding what came first – the chicken or the egg? Firstly, let us find out what lactic acid is, also known as milk acid. It should not be negated without understanding it. To understand lactic acid, we have to understand why and how lactic acid is created. There are two types of energy, anaerobic and aerobic. Aerobic energy relies purely on oxidation and uses Carbohydrates, Fats and Proteins. It is very logical because we receive unlimited amounts of oxygen from the air. Anaerobic energy relies on oxygen free production of energy, hence we can lift something heavy without inhaling deeply first. There are three systems of creating energy:

1. Phosphagen Energy System, which was described earlier, involves ATP and Creatine. The anaerobic system does not require oxygen.

Because of this feature, it is used for short burst exercises e.g. lifting heavy dumbbells.

2.   Glycolysis is the oxidation process of glucose during which it is broken down in to two molecules of Pyrovite, which are further converted into ATP. Glycolysis is an aerobic method, thus it requires oxygen. Energy from this method is used for activities of less than an hour e.g. 30 minutes cardio exercise.

3.   Oxidative Phosphorylation is the oxidation of Carbohydrates, Proteins and Fats to create energy. This method is the most effective of all the methods, but it occurs over many hours.

Ok, now we have enough knowledge to understand lactic acid. When pumping iron in a gym, Phosphagen energy involving Creatine is used for your instantaneous bursts of lifting heavy weights. Phosphagen energy is used in seconds and this is why you have one minute to rest in between. During these seconds, your Glycolysis, which requires oxygen, dramatically reduces because oxygen is more essential for other bodily functions e.g. brain. With the small availability of oxygen, glucose is broken down into two molecules of Pyruvate. As Pyruvate reaches a certain level it is converted into lactic acid. This saves oxygen, which allows Glycolysis to continue breaking down glucose to Pyruvate. As the body returns to a normal state and gains enough oxygen, the lactic acid is reconverted into Pyruvate or reconverted by the liver in to glucose to replenish the glycogen stores in the

muscles and liver. Glycogen is a multibranched molecule for storing energy. It is a little bit like a ball of glucose.

Lactic acid creates an acidic environment and decreases the pH balance in muscles, decreasing the effectiveness of energy production. It tires the muscles and because it is acidic, you can feel a burning sensation during intensive exercises. In the state of acidity your muscles will tire. As I discussed earlier, phosphate Creatine reconverts ADP into ATP, thus the extra supplementation of Creatine makes the whole process more efficient. This reduces the stress on the system. So, yes, Creatine also reduces lactic acid and hence fatigue. There are also other supplements that address this issue in a different way e.g. Beta Alanine

CREATINE AND MUSCLE DEVELOPMENT

There two types of skeletal muscles: Fast and Slow. Slow muscles are used for activities like cardio and fast muscles are used for bodybuilding. A muscular person has well-developed fast muscles. Slow muscles rely on aerobic energy (requiring oxygen). Fast muscles rely on anaerobic energy during which Creatine is terrifically used, hence Creatine specifically helps you to look muscular. Besides Creatine is a strong water-attracting substance, hence it causes your muscles to literally pump up with water and look bigger. You will become heavier because more water is attracted into your muscles. Research has shown that the body weight might increase by as much as 11 pounds (5 kilograms), but do not become alarmed; this is just water, not fat. However, longevity cardio activities like long distance running or endurance cycling do not greatly benefit from Creatine supplementation.

CREATINE AND METHYLATION

Methylation what? Methylation happens in your entire body. It is the simple process of adding or removing a methyl group from different elements in your body. Without going too deep into Chemistry, just think of it as adding or removing a molecule called Methyl. When this addition or removal takes place different hormones and processes are activated or switched off e.g. detoxification process, testosterone, DNA, growth hormone etc.

Any reduction in the stress of the body like supplementing Creatine will save some Methylation. This increases the growth of muscles. It is important to add here that having extra Creatine in your body means you can exercise further and develop your muscles faster. Methylation is useful for repairing your body, hence it is crucial to supplement yourself with Vitamins B6, B9 (also known as Folic acid) and B12 as they greatly help the process, especially in sport. Therefore, if you supplement yourself with Creatine, you reduce the demands for Methylation, but, by exercising

harder, you increase those demands, which can be counteracted by supplementation with B6, B9 and B12. Using Creatine together with the B Vitamins complex aids greatly in increasing your muscle mass. With a deficiency of B Vitamins, hardly any gains in muscle mass are made.

There is also another benefit of Creatine that is often overlooked and not described. As you can see so far, Creatine increases the amount of ATP energy molecules in your muscles, one way or another. In addition, there is a protein called mTOR (Mammalian Target of Rapamycin). This encoded protein is responsible for muscle growth by integrating insulin, hormonal elements and amino acids to create muscles. mTOR does not start unless it can have sufficient levels of ATP, hence Creatine indirectly helps muscle growth through generating enough ATP.

OVERVIEW OF CREATINE

Creatine stimulates muscle growth in several stages:

1.   Initially, muscles grow rapidly because Creatine attracts water into the muscles. This is called Volumizing because the volume of muscle is significantly increased. You must significantly increase your consumption of water to stay well hydrated because Creatine attracts plenty of water. Because you are training heavier, you need even more water. The increase in muscle size causes metabolism to increase as well, thus burning more

fat even when you are asleep. Be warned, you will gain weight because more water is retained in the muscles. Sometimes, you can put on as much as 11 pounds (5 kilograms). However, do not become alarmed, this is water, not fat.

2.   The speed of growth of new muscle increases. This happens because your effort during a workout has increased as Creatine has given you more instant muscle energy.

3.   The speed of growth of new muscle further increases – Creatine attracts more water to your muscles while volumizing. This increases muscle growth because further hydration switches on the biosynthesis of your muscles.

4.   Creatine helps you to maintain the anabolic state of your body. There are two states in which your body can be: anabolic and catabolic. Anabolic state is the state of growth and catabolic state is when your body scavenges all the resource it can find including muscles in order to function properly. Creatine helps during the anabolic state because it relieves the fatigue of the muscles by decreasing the acidity of the muscle, caused by exercise. Creatine has been found to have antioxidant properties. Antioxidants are elements with an extra electron on the orbit which they can give away to another damaged element for repair. Oxidant is the opposite; it does not have a full set of electrons on its orbit so it scavenges your body to gain a full set. An example of an oxidant is alcohol.

5. As it was discussed earlier, Creatine aids Methylation, a process by which different hormones are switched on and off. This is essential for muscle growth.

6. Creatine increases ATP in muscles. In turn, the additional ATP signal mTOR (encoded protein) to initiate muscle growth.

However, research has shown that not everyone responds to Creatine supplementation. Around a quarter of bodybuilders do not respond to Creatine. Sometimes, bodybuilders naturally have high levels of Creatine in their muscles. Unfortunately, in most cases, unresponsiveness to Creatine is due to a wrong diet.

CREATINE'S SIDE EFFECTS

In some people, Creatine causes diarrhea. If you are a member of this club, do not automatically believe forums that suggest your body is not functioning properly and your digestion is bad. It is not natural to take such great quantities of Creatine, hence not everyone is used to it. Sometimes, the body reacts to a previously unseen excess in different ways. It might be an idea to skip the loading phase altogether, reduce the dosages to where your body is fine and then raise the bar and increase Creatine by slowly training your body to become accustomed with the new higher levels of Creatine.

There is another strategy to aid Creatine absorption. This strategy is used in most mixtures of Creatine formulas. It is called Glucose, also known as Dextrose. This works because Glucose causes a spike in insulin production. Insulin is a transporter of Creatine and other amino acids; hence, Creatine is absorbed more efficiently. 10 to 20 grams of glucose is more than enough to cause an insulin spike. Do not worry! You can enjoy your portion of chocolate bar or your small ice cream without concern. Enjoy! However, using this method any other time except after a strenuous workout is very dangerous because, by eating sugary products, in other words glucose, we do cause that insulin spike which can cause Type 2 diabetes when our body cells fail to use insulin correctly. Diabetes is a very dangerous disease during which cells cannot properly use glucose, amino acids and fatty acids. This results in decreased energy and starvation. This also increases the blood sugar levels, which can be fatal. Diabetes also makes the goal of increasing your muscle mass almost impossible because Glycolysis does not work properly, hence nutrients are not transported properly to your muscles. That being said, if you supplement with anything sugary after a strenuous workout, there is nothing to be concerned about because nutrients are supplied to hungry cells during which the nutrients of the cells are replenished and Insulin resistance is not developed. At any other time, avoid consuming large amounts of anything sugary; compromise and reduce it where possible. This also demonstrates that some supplement companies do not consider your interests fully heartedly.

They place plenty of Glucose into Creatine and do not warn you that supplementing at any other time but after a workout puts your body at risk of diabetes. If you want to increase your Creatine absorption at any other time except after a workout, there are alternatives to consuming pure Glucose for when you use supplements not after a strenuous workout e.g. mixing it with more protein powder or eating Carbohydrates like fruit especially banana or using Low GI (slow absorption) Carbohydrates. All of the above increase Insulin in a controlled and healthy fashion.

If everything fails, I suggest it is time to visit your doctor and check your system. Very often diarrhea is caused by sport supplements, if taken incorrectly. Diarrhea indicates high stomach acidity and a simple prescribed pill can solve it or you can take your Creatine with a protein supplement as protein buffers the acid in the stomach. In some cases, it indicates colitis, which is inflammation of the colon. The colon can be inflamed and then water is not absorbed properly, hence this causes diarrhea. In some cases, diarrhea can be a symptom of a stomach infection. In any case, do not self-diagnose, instead visit your doctor. It is your body telling you to visit your doctor.

CREATINE DOSAGES

The first phase in Creatine supplementation is the loading phase. The idea is to load up your muscles to the maximum with Creatine, thus you will increase your Creatine reserves by ten. Research has shown that, after 5 days your Creatine level reaches its maximum, so loading for longer is wasteful and causes unnecessary stress to your body. However, if you are super muscular you obviously have more muscles to nourish, so you might need to prolong the loading phase a little. The opposite applies if you body fat percentage is above average, hence you can reduce your dose. The higher amount of fat you have, the less mass of muscles you have, hence you can decrease your dosage slightly.

After your loading phase, you only need to consume a few grams to maintain your level. You might need to consume a little extra, if you had a heavier workout; hence, your body uses a little extra Creatine. It is also important to take a few grams of Creatine daily because, although Creatine is accumulated in your muscle cells, it leaks from the muscle cells. Around 2 grams of Creatine is lost every day, hence daily supplementation is required when you are building your body.

We all have a different body fat percentage and muscle mass. At the same time your muscles need Creatine, but the rest of the organs do not need it,

hence, depending on your muscle mass you might need different dosages. In short, we need 15 grams of Creatine per every 100 pounds (approx 45 kilograms) of muscle mass. Use the formula below to calculate your approximate Creatine intake, if you are above or below average or if you just want an improved customized loading dosage per day:

Your Weight in Pounds × (100 – Body Fat Percentage) × 0.0015

or

Your Weight in Kilograms × (100 – Body Fat Percentage) × 0.0033

The maintenance dosage is your loading dosage divided by 10 e.g. if your loading dosage is 20 grams then your maintenance dosage will be 20 / 10 = 2 grams per day.

It is important to mention here that extending the loading phase for more than 5 days is counterproductive. After 5 days, Creatine is loaded into your muscles. The extra Creatine will remain in your bloodstream and it would not be absorbed into your muscles. Later on, your kidneys remove over-supplemented Creatine. Hence, extending your loading phase is a waste of money and it puts unnecessary stress on your kidneys.

SKIPPING LOADING PHASE

It is important to keep in mind that Creatine over-supplementation is also possible. Once our muscles reach their highest possible Creatine levels the rest will end up in the toilet. It is wasteful to over-supplement on Creatine. It also causes unnecessary stress on your kidneys and liver. The more unnecessary negative stress your body has, the less efficient your body will be. One of the signs of over-supplementation is diarrhea. As excess Creatine is shifted into your colon, it attracts water which causes diarrhea.

WHEN TO SUPPLEMENT CREATINE

Let us discuss the worst times to supplement Creatine. This is important, so stop listening to opinionated online gurus who do not do their homework and research the subject properly to validate their claims. Do not take Creatine before or during your workout. There are three reasons for this:

1.   It only makes sense to take Creatine before or during your workout only if your Creatine levels are completely depleted. This is very unlikely, if you are supplementing yourself with Creatine already. If you are supplementing yourself with Creatine, you already have a significant amount of Creatine than you would have normally. Once Creatine is in your muscles it is relatively stable and it will not all disappear during a workout

as only tiny amounts will disappear. Supplementing yourself with daily maintenance dosages will fully counteract this.

2.   For Creatine (Cr) to be used by your muscles, it has to be converted into Phosphate Creatine (PCr) first. This process does require energy, thus you will have less energy for the workout itself.

3.   When you consume Creatine, the level of water in your body will change because of creative's water attracting qualities. If you consume Creatine before or during a workout, the level of water will be unbalanced. This causes dehydration, which results in low energy and no muscle development.

The best time to supplement your maintenance dose of Creatine is after a workout because, at this time, your muscles are most sensitive to insulin. Take Creatine with sugars and protein supplements at this time to take advantage of this metabolic window of opportunity. Sugars will increase insulin, which transports all the nutrients into your muscle cells; glucose from sugar replenishes your muscles' glucose reserves, proteins provide building blocks and Creatine is absorbed into your muscles in an effective way.

FORMS OF CREATINE

Supplement companies are constantly trying to surpass their competitors; hence, there are many other forms of Creatine. Some of these forms are Creatine Pyruvate, Tri-Creatine Malate, Creatine Citrate and Creatine Phosphate. Let us dissect these supplements:

1.   Let us look at Creatine Pyruvate and Tri-Creatine Malate. Creatine Pyruvate is a mixture of Pyruvate acid (derived from Glucose) and Creatine Monohydrate (commonly known Creatine). Tri-Creatine Malate is a mixture of Malic acid and Creatine Monohydrate. The issue with these forms of Creatine supplements is that there is virtually no valid controlled research to confirm or disapprove any of their claims. Most of the research on Creatine is on its form as Creatine Monohydrate.

2.   Creatine Citrate refers to different forms of citric acid. It tastes bitter but is more soluble in water. Creatine Citrate is reconverted in to Creatine before it reaches your muscles. Creatine Citrate contains less Creatine itself; hence, it is less economical than Creatine. Again, Creatine Citrate has not been well researched by the scientific community.

3.   Creatine Phosphate is a very expensive form of Creatine and it is wasteful. The idea behind Creatine Phosphate is that Creatine is converted in to Creatine Phosphate in your body for use in your muscles. However, Creatine Phosphate cannot survive outside of the muscle tissues, hence when you consume Creatine Phosphate it is reconverted in to simple

Creatine before it reaches your muscles. In any case, your muscles can absorb Creatine, not Creatine Phosphate. Nothing is gained as you only paid a higher price for a supplement company's hype and false science.

To conclude, take the simple Creatine Monohydrate and save your money. Trust what has been researched properly so far and it is the simple Creatine Monohydrate, which is a reliable supplement. If you want to increase the solubility of simple Creatine, buy micronized Creatine powder which is the same Creatine, only it is finely grated.

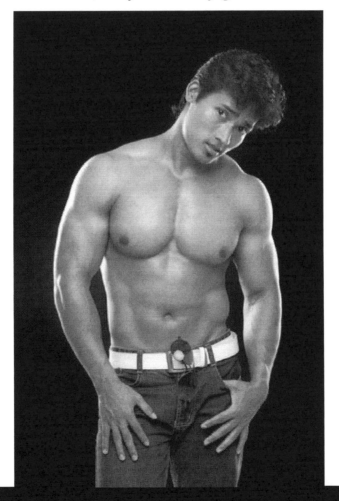

RESUME

Creatine is a combination of three amino acids: Arginine, Glycine and Methionine. It is almost impossible to get high amounts of Creatine from food.

ATP is molecules of energy and the power the body. Creatine regenerates ATP in the muscles.

Creatine fights high muscle acidity, hence it reduces tiredness.

Creatine mainly aids the fast twitch muscles, i.e. the ones that make you look muscular and allow you to lift heavy objects.

Creatine attracts water into the muscles making them look bigger and increasing overall weight of bodybuilders. Because of Creatine's high absorbability of water, you must significantly increase water consumption to remain hydrated.

Creatine is often used during a period of hard workouts during which plenty of oxidative stresses occur. To protect yourself from these stresses, consume Vitamins B6, B9 and B12.

Creatine indirectly influences many processes which trigger muscle growth.

You can get diarrhea because of Creatine, if it is of low quality or it is not fully absorbed and the remainder attracts water to your colon. Try to reduce the dosage or consume a higher quality Creatine. Taking it with something sugary can remedy the situation because of the insulin spike. Use it only during very short loading periods or straight after exercises because prolonged use of sugar leads to Type 2 Diabetes.

Roughly, the dosage is 25 grams over a day for 5 days during the loading phase and then 3 grams daily. If you cannot bear the loading, consider omitting the loading phase altogether.

Micronized Creatine powder from respectable labs is recommended, as it is the best and most researched.

HMB

HMB (Beta-Hydroxy Beta-Methyl Butyric acid) is derived from the essential amino acid Leucine. Leucine is one of the most essential acids for humans. In the body, only 5% of Leucine is converted into HMB. HMB started its popularity contest for the hearts and minds of bodybuilders from the 1990s.

HMB's efficiency is constantly debated. Many studies show that it helps to prevent protein breakdown and increases muscle mass. In simple words, it preserves your muscles and further increases your muscles. However, some studies were mainly conducted on sedentary people. Many so-called fitness supplement gurus picked on this. They state that it has not been proven to work for physically active people, thus save your money. If only they researched further, they would have found that some research was carried out on physically active people. Through over six weeks of supplementation with HMB, runners experienced a 58% decrease in muscle damage than those who did not supplement themselves with HMB. Early research has demonstrated fantastic results as some individuals gained as much as 1.2 kg (2.6 lbs) of lean muscle tissue. HMB also improves protein synthesis by 20%, especially in older people. Further research has shown that HMB increased the lactic acid threshold of cyclists. In simple words, your general acidity and H+ ions decrease and you can work out for longer. All of these results decrease the body's fat

because it uses less protein for energy; instead it uses more fat for energy. Additionally, the metabolic rate increases because of an increase in muscle tissue.

Yes, HMB has been proven more effective for less trained people and less effective for well-trained people, but so what? If HMB is still useful and you have the money, then use it. Yes, HMB has a relatively high price tag, but, come on, a gain of up to 1.2 kg (2.6 lbs) in lean muscle tissue, even on a calorie deficit diet and exercise is superb. It almost seems to be a miracle; many think it is impossible to gain muscle whilst losing weight.

Why not to take Leucine instead because HMB is derived from Leucine? There are two points to the answer:
1.   The studies have demonstrated that the desired effect is achieved only after consuming at least 3 grams of HMB daily, and the need is higher for physically active people, like you and me, who go to the gym regularly. You have to consume plenty of Leucine to convert enough into HMB as only 5% of Leucine is converted into HMB.
2.   Even if you somehow manage to get enough Leucine in your diet as a supplement and your stomach does not protest against, even then it is not guaranteed that there are enough digestive enzymes to convert that small amount of Leucine into HMB.

How exactly does HMB works? The exact mechanism is still not known. The most likely theory is that HMB may increase levels of good cholesterol, also known as HDL (high density lipoprotein). Do not confuse HDL cholesterol with bad cholesterol, which everyone is fighting against. Bad cholesterol is also known as LDL (Low Density Lipoprotein). LDL cholesterol clogs up your arteries and causes many complications. Heart attack is commonly associated with LDL cholesterol – the bad one. HDL cholesterol is essential for your body in many ways. Let us focus on muscle cells. Muscle cells have cell membranes like other cells to contain themselves. As you exercise hard or diet, these membranes are damaged and hard-gained protein leaks out. Fear not, because HDL cholesterol – the good guy, patches up the leaks because that is what these membranes are mainly made of. HDL cholesterol also decreases LDL cholesterol. The lesson here is that not all cholesterol is bad for you.

Another research has investigated the influence of HMB when taken together with Creatine. This research has demonstrated that combining HMB and Creatine increased the size of lean muscle and strength.

How much should you take it? The body produces 0.2 to 0.4g of HMB. 10g to 20g of Creatine and 3g of HMB were found to be most effective. Reduce Creatine after a loading period to 2 to 3 g a day.

RESUME

HMB is derived from the essential amino acid Leucine. HMB is rare in the body because only 5% of it is made from Leucine; hence, direct supplementation of HMB is advised.

HMB preserves your muscles and reduces the tiredness of your muscles. It is especially useful for older bodybuilders. HMB's overall anabolic qualities increase muscle mass and metabolism and reduce fat.

HMB is highly recommended for bodybuilders who are slimming down because it prevents the loss of muscles with fat.

Consuming Creatine and HMB is a good idea because the effect of it is compounding and beneficial for bodybuilders.

The recommended dosage of HMB is 3 grams per day.

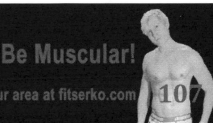

LEUCINE

Leucine is one of the essential amino acids, which your body cannot produce by itself. Leucine is one of the most abundant amino acids in the body.

Leucine is mostly used during dieting or cutting period (where you lose fat covering a muscular physique). It is very simple to understand why. Leucine is eventually converted into HMB (Beta-Hydro Beta-Methyl Butyrate) and HMB is fantastic for saving your muscle mass from disappearing while on a diet. Understand this! When you lose weight you may think you mainly lose fat, but this perception is a far cry from the truth. In normal conditions nearly half of the weight you lose is from your muscle mass. A lot of it is water and only around 30% to 40% is actual fat. Note: Water constitutes most of the body, but the understanding becomes complicated when you lose weight because water is also in the muscles, fat and even bones. When you lose weight you alter your proportion of water. In simple words, your fat and muscles become dryer; imagine dried fruit or beef jerky. Anyhow, HMB protects muscles and makes sure you just lose fat, to avoid repetition please read the chapter on HMB in this book to understand the full spectrum of benefits and action. If you have not yet read that chapter, please do it now before continuing. It is necessary to fully understand Leucine.

However, all of the results of HMB, which is produced from Leucine are good, but only for one function – only 5% of Leucine is converted into HMB, hence it is more economical to supplement with HMB to increase it in your body rather than supplementing with Leucine to increase your HMB levels.

Leucine is still used as a supplement in spite of the fact HMB is more effective in protecting muscle mass from decreasing while dieting. The impact of Leucine is 10 times greater on protein synthesis in your body than any other amino acid. Leucine activates so-called mTOR (mammalian target of Rapamycin – encoded protein) which regulates muscle growth in your body (or in other words regulates protein synthesis). mTOR integrates amino acids, insulin and hormonal elements to create muscle. When you have low Leucine levels in your blood it directly signals to mTOR to stop muscle growth because there are not enough amino acids in the body for muscular growth.

In fact, because of this assertion, some supplement stores portray Leucine as the legal supplement closest to anabolic steroids. I hope you read and understood enough of this book to realize that this statement is absolutely rubbish. Well, yes, Leucine is required (which is one of the most abundant amino acids in the body anyway) for muscle growth. Well, so is water, so is air for breathing... Too many supplement companies do describe the effects of the supplement correctly, but fail to mention, in spite of such a vivid picture, that you do not really need to supplement with a particular substance.

There are only two cases where supplementation with Leucine actually makes sense:

1.   When you workout very hard and take Leucine during or after a strenuous workout. This is because Leucine is absorbed directly into the muscles and not by the liver. This makes it a perfect source of protein during high demanding periods of intense workouts such as working out so intensely that you want to vomit. Leucine, one of the most abundant amino acids in your body, is actually needed in larger amounts when you put huge stresses on your body. However, it does not make sense to supplement, if you do not exercise that intensely. If you do not exercise that intensely, taking Leucine will have some benefits; it will not poison you or interfere with your bodily functions, but it will be a waste of money.

2.   The second case in which Leucine is beneficial is when you are on a very strict diet. To be precise, when you are on a diet that supplies only half of the calories required for normal bodily functions. If such diets are effective is another question. Personally, I think such diets are a useless waste of effort and time. This topic about suitable diets for a bodybuilder's needs is a huge topic for another book which one day I hope to write. So if you are on a highly restrictive diet, then, yes, do supplement with Leucine, but it is better to find another diet more suitable for a bodybuilder.

Okay, I have explained the benefits of Leucine and in which cases to take it. However, I recommend against it because there are other more effective ways. That being said, 2.5 grams of Leucine is normally taken before a workout, 5 gram during a workout and then followed by 5 grams of Leucine added to a post workout drink. Some bodybuilders take an extra 5 grams of Leucine before sleeping in the hope of encouraging more efficient muscle growth. Those who are on a strict diet can consume 2.5 grams of Leucine with restrictive calorie meals and in between them.

Now, let me give you the main reason why buying Leucine, although not a waste of money, is a very inefficient way of spending your money at the least. Leucine is also present in a supplement called BCAA (Branch Chained Amino Acids) which contains Leucine, Isoleucine and Valine all of which are amino acids. When these three amino acids are taken together, they are proven more effective than if taken separately. Therefore, to simplify it, let us suppose, for your body to take full advantage of Leucine, you need to take it with other two amino acids, namely Isoleucine and Valine. Please, refer to the next chapter about BCAA for when to take it and what are its benefits.

RESUME

Leucine although essential is a most abundant amino acid; 5% of it breaks down in to HMB. Leucine activates the coded mTOR protein that initiates muscle growth.

Leucine is recommended for when you are on a diet to lose weight. This is due to the qualities of HMB because only 5% of Leucine is converted into HMB, hence it is more effective and economical to supplement with HMB instead.

Leucine is recommended when you workout hard and frequently – 5 or more times a week during which you sweat like mad.

The dosages for Leucine are 2.5 grams before a workout, 5 grams during a workout and then followed by 5 grams post workout. For those on a strict diet, the dosage is 2.5 grams between meals.

It is more efficient to get Leucine from BCAAs or protein shakes rather than on its own.

BCAAS

You may ask what are amino acids? Amino acids are blocks of protein and proteins are the building blocks for your muscles. Essential amino acids cannot be produced by our bodies, hence they must be obtained from food and supplements. Our bodies can produce Non-essential amino acids; hence, there is hardly a need to supplement. BCAA – Branch Chained Amino Acids – consist of three amino acids: Leucine, Isoleucine and Valine. They are all essential amino acids. We can gain BCAA only through supplements and food.

Scientific research proved that BCAA enhances the performance of bodybuilders. You can complete more weight lifting sets and lift heavier weights. BCAA also increases muscle growth.

BCAAs are great for bodybuilders. BCAAs are metabolized directly in the muscles, not the liver. This is much quicker and allows direct absorption on demand. BCAAs are essential for more muscle growth. You need new proteins to build muscles. BCAAs are also great for athletes because it gives them instant energy for better performance.

During training, BCAAs provide as much as 15% of the energy. This is amazing for a few caps of BCAAs. For this reason exactly, it is important to

take BCAAs at the correct time – during training. BCAAs also reduce the depletion of glycogen in your body during a workout. Glycogen is stored in the muscles for energy. Glycogen is Carbohydrate based. You need Glycogen to train. If your Glycogen is depleted, your muscles suffer.

To put it simply, BCAAs reduce overtraining and fatigue. This is how BCAAs enhance the performance of bodybuilders. Because BCAAs are the building blocks for muscles, they are beneficial if you want to become ripped.

It is also important to take BCAAs, if you are on Carbohydrate restricting diet. BCAAs reduce muscle loss during dieting. BCAAs simply maintain your muscles by feeding them directly.

In the case of BCAAs, supplement companies underestimate the required dosages of BCAAs. This is very unusual which may be due to the expensive manufacturing process. If they recommend larger dosages it is beyond the consumers' pockets. Supplement companies normally encourage over-supplementation, so they can sell more supplements. I consume 30 to 50 grams during a workout. Distribute the dose over the period of your workout. Anything less is a waste of BCAAs and money. However, if you have a plenty of spare cash, you can take 20 grams before a workout, 20 grams during a workout and 20 grams immediately after a

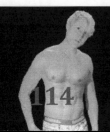

workout. You do not need to take it during the day or between meals unless you are on a diet that severely restricts nutrients. It is better to take BCAAs on the empty stomach to avoid competition for absorption.

Recent research has demonstrated that Leucine is one of the most important amino acids. The proportion of these three amino acids is a portion of Leucine, a portion of Isoleucine and a portion of Valine. According to recent research in support of Leucine, you get BCAA powder with 8 portions of Leucine, 1 portion of Isoleucine and 1 portion of Valine. Hence, from the different types of BCAAs, choose the ones with higher Leucine content. Because Leucine has became more popular, the wholesale price of Leucine for manufacturers has increased, hence some of them have increased the amount of Isoleucine or Valine and not changed the amount of Leucine; avoid these supplements and consider them as false economy. It is important to understand which ingredient is the most expensive in the mix, if you do not want to be duped.

BCAAs come in the forms of powder and capsules. I prefer capsules because it is convenient. However, the capsules are sometimes three times the price of the powder. The powder itself does not mix easily with water as it solidifies. There are water friendly versions on the market of course, at a premium price. With this type of BCAA powder, I make an ice-slush. I mix the BCAA powder with water, sugar free cordial and ice in an ice crusher.

However, I have to make the BCAA ice-slush a couple of minutes before leaving for the gym to avoid the degradation of BCAAs. Even in its powder form, it is very expensive considering that you need higher dosages than the ones recommended on the labels to achieve results you can see and feel. There is another option, if you still want capsules. You can buy a capping kit with which you can create capsules with your preferred dosage and mix.

RESUME

BCAAs consist of Leucine, Isoleucine and Valine. BCAAs enhance performance and increase muscle growth. BCAAs are metabolized directly in the muscles. During training, BCAAs provide as much as 15% of the energy. BCAAs also reduce the depletion of Glycogen. Consume BCAAs, if you are on a carbohydrate-restricted diet.

Chose BCAAs with a higher Leucine content as Leucine is the most important element.

The recommended dose is 30 to 50 grams distributed over the workout. Surprisingly, supplement companies recommend lesser dosages.

BETA ALANINE

BENEFITS OF BETA ALANINE

Beta Alanine is a slightly different amino acid from Alanine; however, as soon as a formula changes even slightly, all of the effects change too. Beta Alanine is normally created in your own body from peptides such as Carnosine. Beta Alanine combines with Histidine to increase the peptide called Carnosine (Beta-Alanyl-L-Histidine). Carnosine maintains a healthy pH balance of the body. In simple words, it prevents the body from becoming acidic; hence, muscle recovery increases, because the tiredness of the muscles is due to the presence of acid in them.

Let us have a detailed look at how Beta Alanine works. To understand this, we have to approach from afar. I will try to be as simple as possible. During training, you use two systems, Cardio/Aerobic Energy (based on oxygen) and Anaerobic for weightlifting, based on inner cellular energy production through ATP molecules (Adenosine Triphosphate). During these processes, energy is released and this extra energy helps to form ATP (the energy molecule). Pyruvate is further used in different aspects of energy production but let us leave that for now. What we are looking at here is $H+$. $H+$ is a chemical sign for an hydrogen ion. A hydrogen atom has one proton in its nucleus and one electron circling around the nucleus. A hydrogen atom transforms into $H+$ when this circling electron is removed.

Now, the hydrogen is missing one electron (in other words it is positively charged, H+), hence the atoms wants to take an electron by force from other atoms. This is a free radical (a guy that destroys others or in other words acidic). On top of this process, while this energy molecule ATP is used, it produces H+ again; hence even more H+ free radicals are in your body. The pH balance is the measure of the amount of H+ radical atoms. Be careful here when you do your own research. H+ is only at the first phase. It can transform into many other acidic molecules, hence some sources can confuse you by stating that the pH level is a measure of H+ derivatives e.g. Hydronium H3O+ and many others. All is true but, in essence, it is all initially H+. It is at a specific level of the pH balance that your muscles can operate: if the pH balance of your muscles is too acidic, you will be exhausted and you body will be torn apart for nutrients to feed the body. If the pH balance of your muscles is too alkaline, there will be no sufficient chemical reactions for your muscles to work. Do not be concerned with the too alkaline levels of pH. It is a physical impossibility until one is dead. During exercise, you change your pH balance into exhaustion territory. Yes, it is dealt with by numerous processes and the body will alkalize the pH itself, but it will take some time. Here, a good helper comes, Beta Alanine. It is converted into Carnosine by your body and Carnosine reacts with H+ and absorbs it. It serves as a buffer against high H+ levels.

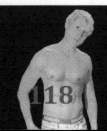

The effectiveness of Beta Alanine in decreasing muscle acidity is a well-researched and proven fact of science. The good news is that Beta Alanine has been researched on humans, not on rats or any other animals. Sometimes, what is tested on rats does not happen in humans. It is proven that, by taking Beta Alanine, you will:

- Increase your strength
- Increase your muscle mass
- Increase cardio stamina
- Increase weightlifting stamina
- Decrease fatigue

Beta Alanine is sometimes used when you do all the right things and you get stuck at a plateau, then you can supplement with Beta Alanine to push yourself further. It is well worth trying, provided that you not only think the things you do are correct, but they are correct in reality.

If you read the previous paragraphs attentively, you might have noticed that naturally Beta Alanine is created by your body from Carnosine. Beta Alanine is consumed to increase Carnosine, so the final goal is to increase Carnosine in your blood, not Beta Alanine. This brings the question – so why not supplement with Carnosine in the first place? Well, the answer is that our bodies have their own way of dealing with nutrients and elements. Firstly, there is normally plenty of Histidine in your body, so, by adding Beta

Alanine, you help your body to create more Carnosine in your blood. Secondly, "in your blood" is the key here. Your digestive system breaks down Carnosine, which you consume. Afterwards, only around 60% of it is converted back into Carnosine in your blood, thus 40 % is lost. Now add the first and the second reasons:

1. There is plenty of Histidine in the body and Carnosine is made for the body's use by combining Histidine and Beta Alanine, not by taking them directly.

2. If you consume Carnosine, just over half of it is absorbed into your blood which is much less in comparison to Beta Alanine. Most of the beta Alanine is mixed with Histidine, thus producing Carnosine in your blood.

3. Beta Alanine supplement is more effective and efficient than Carnosine supplement, looking at the increase of Carnosine in the blood, which delivers elements to your muscles.

Supplementing with beta Alanine for 12 weeks has been proven to increase Cartosine's availability for muscle use by a whopping 80%. Even 4 weeks is enough to increase it by up to 65%. Beta Alanine is a great supplement for both aerobic and anaerobic activities (in other words for cardio and weightlifting). There are two types of muscle fibers: Type 1 Slow is for

cardio and Type 2 Fast is for weightlifting. Type 1 Slow muscle fibers produce energy through the use of oxygen (hence longer lasting) and Type 2 Fast muscle fibers produce energy through metabolic processes without oxygen (hence fast acting and quickly depleted). To be precise, there are two Type 2 muscle fibers: Type 2a and Type 2b. Type 2a is a mixture of Type 1 and Type 2b which produces energy using oxygen and through inner metabolic processes. Beta Alanine is effective for both types; however, it is even more effective for Type 2 muscles, hence, because you are a bodybuilder, your main effort is lifting weights, hence you gain even more.

Research has demonstrated a 16% increase of durability on a bicycle. In other words, using Beta almandine properly is like extending your workout by an extra 16%. Of course, only if you workout intensively enough and invest closer to 100% of your workout time to muscles and not socializing. Let us see what that means if you visit a gym 5 times a week for cardio and weightlifting workouts for a maximum of 50 minutes:

50 minutes × 16% increase = 58 minutes (8 minutes extra)

Then... there are around 261 Monday to Fridays. Okay, you will miss some days due to holidays etc. Let us say you will miss a whole month and will visit a gym 240 times a year.

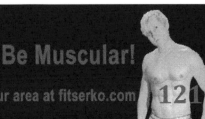

This means...

8 minutes extra (16% increase) × 240 visits a year = extra 1920 minutes of a workout (or 32 hours or extra 38.4 gym visits a year) just from consuming Beta Alanine. This is considering the 16% increase during a cardio activity. The effect of Beta Alanine is even higher for weightlifting activities. Do you begin to see the potential of correct supplementation? Moreover, what is it about other supplements and compounding increase? I believe that with correct supplementation you literally replace 2 years of exercise in a gym without supplements for 1 year with supplements. Do not be fooled by a "Magic Pill" idea in your head. Supplements will only work if you workout hard and correctly, diet well and only then will they work. Without correct workouts and a correct diet, any supplement will not work and will be just a waste. You might as well go and make funky wallpaper out of the money you spent on supplements.

Nevertheless, hang on, we have not finished on Beta Alanine yet, oh no. Beta Alanine significantly increases the levels of Carnosine, which in it turn:

- Is a potent antioxidant that fights free radicals that destroy the body from the inside

- Can appose so-called Glycation, which is suspected of accelerating aging; however, more research needs to be done in this area. Glycation

occurs when blood sugar is bonded with protein and fat cells without the participation of enzymes, hence not where it is needed and it is unintended.

-        Is a potent chelant, you might wonder - what the heck? Chelant is an antioxidant on steroids. Normally, free radicals have only one electron missing, but some metals have free radicals with 2 electrons missing. Well, Carnosine can neutralize such a metal-based free radical by reacting with it. Not all antioxidants can do that. Carnosine helps your body to detoxify itself from toxic forms of metal in your body. A similar process outside the human body happens with lime scale in your bathroom. You can apply a solution to remove it.

Because of all the various properties of Carnosine, it is used in anti-aging therapies and even in some cosmetics and beauty salons. Beta Alanine seems to be the most optimal way to increase Carnosine in your blood, hence Beta Alanine is often used regardless of how hard you train.

BETA ALANINE, ENERGY DRINKS AND PRE-WORKOUT SUPPLEMENTS

Beta Alanine is transported into your body by Sodium (also known as Natrium; its chemical sign is Na) and Chloride (chemical sign is Cl). Sodium and Chloride are in your diet in the form of NaCl (Sodium Chloride) which is common salt. Beta Alanine's transport means that without sodium and chloride, Beta Alanine will not be absorbed. This is why during a period of workouts it is recommended not to decrease your salt levels in your diet. Of course, no one can recommend taking excessive salt because the modern diet already offers salt levels that are too high. High salt levels are responsible for high blood pressure, which causes around 7.6 million premature deaths. This figure will increase in future as the population grows and a bigger proportion of the world's population adopts modern fast food diets.

However, Sodium and Chloride are not the exclusive Beta Alanine's transporters; they are transporters for many amino acids and their derivatives, but Taurine has a special place. Taurine is a non-essential, and made by the body. It has not been mentioned previously because it is primarily for brain development rather than bodybuilding, although it does have some benefits for the heart and muscles. Taurine seriously inhibits Beta Alanine's production because of Taurine's direct and potent

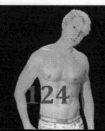

competition for the same transport (Sodium and Chloride). I do not know if you noticed, but Taurine is the most frequent ingredient in energy drinks and pre-workout solutions. Many bodybuilders use these pre-workout solutions, energy drinks and even Taurine on its own to increase the motivation levels during a hard workout in the gym. Well, do not use those solutions because they inhibit the absorption of Beta Alanine. Because beta Alanine cannot do its job; the pH balance is becoming acidic. Your muscles become tired, although you might not feel tired because of Taurine and caffeine your muscles are tired which means they will break down to be consumed for energy and you will not recover soon enough. Muscles grow during a period of rest and not during exercise. Muscles are provoked into growth during exercise. If your muscles are tired and not recovered from exercise, they will not grow and will not turn on the anabolic switch which allows muscle growth. So remember, no energy drinks or pre-workout solutions that contain high levels of Taurine.

HOW TO TAKE BETA ALANINE

The usual dosage for beta Alanine is 3 grams a day, so far there is no evidence that Beta Alanine is toxic to the liver and hence can be taken for very long periods. Some bodybuilders still cycle it and have a couple of weeks break every 12 weeks. Cycling is a good idea for anything, even Vitamins. One of the reasons is to avoid the stagnation of your body through becoming used to something too much. Because of the immediate impact of Beta Alanine and a strong 'pins and needles' sensation it gives, it also creates a psychological impact. You feel it works; hence, the placebo effect helps even more. I use Beta Alanine before the exercise and I can feel how the 'pins and needles' sensation dissipated more if I train harder. It is a kind of a guide for me to know if I have pushed my body enough, because I personally do not like this sensation. I am encouraged to workout hard to get rid of it faster. On the other hand, if you like the sensation you might look forward to exercising because of beta Alanine's buzz, so play to your own advantage and your own perceptions. Almost everyone feels this sensation and everyone of those feels it to a different degree. Some do not feel it at all. In any case, Beta Alanine is normally taken before the exercise because that is when your body will need it most, some take it during and straight after a workout. As mentioned before, do not take it with energy drinks and pre-workout supplements containing Taurine. Beta Alanine is better than those dangerous energy drinks and its components in some pre-workout formulas. Beta Alanine's benefits appear within just 1 to 2 weeks. It is worth mentioning that do not take beta Alanine only as a pre-workout supplement. The biggest benefits from Beta Alanine come when you supplement with it regularly to build up your Carnosine levels. It is also known that Vitamin E, Alpha Lipoic Acid and N-Acetyl-Cysteine (NAC) help Beta Alanine further in its work. All of these three elements are available as supplements and are beneficial in their own rights.

One particular combination of Beta Alanine has been recently research and has promising results for athletic performance; it is Creatine. The use of both has a synergetic affect where 2 + 2 = 5. Creatine regenerates ATP and Beta Alanine buffers extra H+ from extra ATP being used. Let us suppose your performance can be measured as a number of 100. On its own, Beta Alanine will increase it by 16% which will make your performance figure 116. Suppose Creatine will increase your performance by 20% that means, on its own, it will increase that 100% performance figure to 120%. Some people think that the extra 16% from beta Alanine and 20% from Creatine will increase performance by 16 + 20 = 36 to 136, this is not correct in the case of Beta Alanine and Creatine together. Because Beta Alanine and Creatine are synergetic (rely directly on each other). We will see a compounding effect increased that 100 to 139.2 (which is 100 increased by 16% and then the resulting 116 increasing by further 20%). However, mathematics does not always work for body processes and, in reality, the synergetic impact of Creatine and Beta Alanine is found to be even greater than just a compounding multiplication. Studies have found that the synergetic use of Creatine and Beta Alanine increases muscle mass creates more energy and decreases fat significantly more than on their own as they enhance each other. In the studies, they used a mixture of 1.6 grams a day of Beta Alanine and 5.25 grams a day of Creatine. If you attentively read the paragraphs before, you might have noticed that recommended dosage for Beta Alanine is 3 grams a day, and Creatine's usual maintenance dosage is from 2 to 3 grams a day (except when loading with 20 to 30 grams a day for the first 5 days). Well, do not be confused. Remember you are a hard-working bodybuilder and your body requirements are different from the body requirements of an average person. It is near impossible at present to calculate all the synergetic impacts of your lifestyle, genetics, all the supplements, all the foods and all the exercise you take. It is a good idea to stick to individually recommended dosages; it might not be the best idea, but it is the most feasible.

RESUME

Beta Alanine is derived from the amino acid Alanine. Beta Alanine is combined with Histidine in the body to create Carnosine, which reduces muscle acidity, thus reducing the tiredness of the body. Histidine is plentiful in the body; hence, there is no need to supplement. It is more efficient to take Beta Alanine and not Carnosine. Beta Alanine is one the most powerful anti-oxidants that fights the signs of old age.

The compounding effect of Beta Alanine over a long period of time and further compounding through combining with other supplements means that you can save time significantly and reach your bodybuilding goals faster. Beta Alanine is often mixed with Creatine to enhance each other effects.

Avoid pre-workout and energy drinks containing Taurine, which inhibits Beta Alanine. Salt in the diet is needed to transport the nutrients to the muscles, if you workout hard however, you have to balance it out and be moderate in the consumption of salt because of the risk of salt related illnesses.

Be aware, you will probably experience the sensation of pricking needles on your skin while taking Beta Alanine.

Take 3 grams a day for 12 weeks and have a break for a couple of weeks.

GLUTAMINE

Glutamine, also known as L-glutamine, is a conditionally essential amino acid. Glutamine is not a miracle supplement, but it can be very useful. The science behind glutamine is strong. Glutamine is reliable and well studied. Glutamine is great for preventing overtraining. While you train hard, glutamine is depleted from your body. When glutamine is depleted, the recovery time of your muscles increases. If your muscles do not recover fast, the growth of your muscles is compromised. Additionally, when you exercise hard, your immune system is compromised, as glutamine is essential for the multiplication of our white blood cells, which fight off viruses and bacteria. In fact, without glutamine, the cells of your immune system (white blood cells) are severely compromised. There is another great quality of glutamine. It volumizes your muscle cells by attracting water to them, which hydrates your muscles and makes them appear larger, and increases your fat-burning metabolic rate to uncover that tantalizing six pack. The effect of attracting water is similar to that of Creatine. Read the chapter on Creatine for more information.

Our bodies can produce non-essential amino acids; hence, there is hardly a need to supplement with them. However, if the amino acid is conditionally essential, i.e. our bodies cannot rapidly produce it while you train hard. This is why you have to take glutamine as a supplement during training. I must warn you that glutamine is useful only if you train hard! Glutamine is one of the most abundant amino acids in your blood and is depleted only during hard training. Glutamine needs replenishing during intensive training.

Another reason for taking Glutamine is to prevent muscle breakdown. Muscle breakdown happens when your energy needs are so high that your hard-earned muscles are burnt for energy. Glutamine stops this. In any case, if your body fat is above 9%, your body will mainly burn fat and will not burn muscles. Therefore, glutamine is useful in preventing the breakdown of muscle only if you are skinny or already moderately fit. Remember, the main benefit of glutamine is to stop overtraining. Avoiding muscle breakdown is an extra benefit for those with less than 10% body fat. Those who have 10% and above of body fat will not burn muscles to a great extent.

There many opinions on when to take Glutamine. Some people take glutamine in the morning to increase growth hormones. Growth hormones are beneficial for muscle growth. Studies have shown a 400% increase in growth hormones, if you take glutamine in the morning. It also increases growth hormone if taken before sleep, 5 grams of glutamine before sleep is advisory. Growth hormones are essential for muscle growth just like testosterone. Although growth hormones in adults are significantly lower than in teenagers and increasing it, even by several times, will not make

you taller. It is still a good idea to increase growth hormone levels when you workout because most of your body's reserves of nutrient and hormones are depleted. Some take glutamine before a workout to buffer up with nutrients. In my opinion,this is useless. Much of the glutamine is wasted just before it is needed. Some take glutamine during training to top up the reserves of glutamine as you train. Some take glutamine after a workout to help recovery. This is the best strategy. Some take glutamine before sleep to increase growth hormones and provide nutrients to repair muscles, especially if you train in the evenings.

This is how most people make a mistake, over-supplementation and waste money. Because of glutamine's various benefits, it is easy for supplement companies to mislead you and make you take it at least five times a day. They would like you to believe you waste your muscles for energy just by walking. The more you consume the more they sell.

My advice is save your money, take it after your workout. This is the best time to take 3 to 5 grams of glutamine. You can take 3 to 5 grams of glutamine before sleep, if you want. If you really want, you can take 3 to 5 grams during a workout. However, you will benefit from glutamine the most and save your money, if you take it only once – after a hard workout.

RESUME

Glutamine, a conditionally essential amino acid, prevents overtraining, aids the immune system, volumizes and hydrates muscles. Glutamine is one of the most abundant amino acids in the body, but it cannot be rapidly produced by our bodies when training hard and only then it is useful, otherwise it is a waste of effort and money.

If glutamine is taken first in the morning or before sleep, it increases the growth hormones.

To prevent muscle breakdown, glutamine supplement is recommended only for the already fit and slim. For those with more than 10% of fat, it is not needed.

It is easy to over-supplement with glutamine. Take 3 to 5 grams post workout and 3 to 5 grams before sleep.

LYSINE

Lysine is an essential amino acid, which we cannot make in our body, thus we must gain it from our food. However, this chapter will be short because it is more effective to supplement with protein shakes as supplementing with lysine is like splitting hairs. The reason I decided to write about Lysine in a separate chapter is that it is sold separately in many fitness stores so I am trying to be comprehensive. In addition, I want to explain that you will not find all the supplements described in here because most of them are just amino acids supplied in protein powders and they were covered in chapters on protein powders.

Lysine is essential for your body to absorb calcium, which is essential for the strength of your bones. The stronger your bones are, the less likelihood of a gym related injury occurring. Someone recovering from an injury can benefit from it. Lysine is also used to treat cold sores so, if your suffering from cold sores, you might want to supplement yourself with Lysine. Lysine is essential for protein synthesis, it protects from overtraining, helps in hormone production and maintains nitrogen levels. Nitrogen levels determine if your muscles are in the growing stage or stagnant, but none of that is surprising because that is what all amino acids do. We need all of them, it is called food. So do not waste your money or buy it just because they sell it separately. If you want to increase your amino acids to build muscles, buy a good quality protein powder (see chapters on protein powders to understand the differences between protein powders). Some supplement companies claim that Lysine promotes the production of testosterone but a study has not confirmed this. Just because Lysine is essential for hormones production, it does not increase it. Here is one "supplement" you cannot live without, oxygen. I will not go any further and say, "breathe more air to be more alive". So, please, ignore those bogus claims about Lyisine. It is not separate from other amino acids and it is beneficial in protein supplements and in diet. Yet, I have to detail the dosage for separate consumption by a bodybuilder. The dosage of lysine is 1 to 2 grams daily. Some excessively consume it and, because it does not have known negative impacts, they mega supplement with it. If they take more than 15 grams of Lysine, they might suffer from stomach cramps.

RESUME

Lysine is an essential amino acid. It is most effective in protein shakes. Lysine is required to absorb Calcium, essential for muscle growth, aids recovery and maintains nitrogen levels, which promotes muscle growth and participates in hormone production.

Get Lysine from your diet or protein shakes. If you decide to supplement separately with Lysine, 2 grams a day is recommended. Dosages of over 15 grams are known to cause stomach cramps.

ZMA

ZMA stands for Zinc Monomethionine Aspartate, Magnesium Aspartate and vitamin B6. Simply, it is a combination of zinc, magnesium and vitamin B6. It is claimed to raise your testosterone levels naturally. I can confirm that, compared to other so-called natural testosterone boosters, ZMA is more superior and is often overlooked. The names of other less effective supplements contain parts of the word "testosterone" for marketing purposes.

ZMA has many other good qualities. It increases your endurance, so you can exercise properly for maximum impact on your muscles. You recover sooner, so your muscles grow quicker and you can have more productive gym sessions. It also helps you to stay hydrated reducing the likelihood of workout stalling cramps. Another quality of ZMA is that it helps you have deeper sleeps, so you can wake up refreshed and recovered ready for more. Zinc is necessary for many body functions. For bodybuilders, they are energy, muscle growth and liver protection. You do need to protect your liver when you take a variety of different supplements and put your body under stress. Zinc is known to be absorbed better without anything acidic, hence avoid taking it with Vitamin C, orange juice, or anything acidic. Magnesium is great for the heart and your heart fitness level determines how hard you can work out in a gym. Magnesium also supports a good

balance of Potassium and Sodium. You need both of them to be hydrated. Your muscles cannot develop without proper hydration as everything will shut down as you can only live three to five days without water. It is essential for everyone to take zinc and magnesium because magnesium deficiency is one of the most common deficiencies and zinc deficiency is one of the most common in the modern world. Let us go further and see why we need Vitamin B6 in a ZMA mix. Vitamin B6 helps absorption, helps magnesium to regulate your mood and induces deeper sleep. It also helps protein synthesis, also known as muscle growth.

Study after study has confirmed that ZMA raises testosterone. It does slightly raise the levels of growth hormones, but the level of testosterone rises further. Glutamine is more effective in raising the level of growth hormones; see the chapter on glutamine for further information on this. ZMA is a natural supplement for raising your levels of testosterone, which you need to switch on your muscle growth into accelerated mode. ZMA has also been reported to increase strength by an amazing 2.5 times and it is natural, so there is no need to cycle it.

ZMA's zinc, magnesium and vitamin B6 proportions vary from manufacturer to a manufacturer; however, the studies on ZMA mainly used 30 mg of zinc, 450 mg of magnesium and 11 mg of Vitamin B6. With this knowledge, you can now save at least 50% on purchases of ZMA. Just go to a

supermarket or a drug store and buy Zinc, Magnesium and Vitamin B6 separately.

You also need to take ZMA because of regular exercise, as your Zinc levels decrease sharply. You do need it to produce testosterone to increase your muscle mass, hence taking ZMA is crucial to a person who physically looks after himself.

Avoid taking ZMA with calcium because it inhibits the absorption of Zinc. However, the amount of calcium has to be significant to inhibit zinc absorption. There is a limited research which indicates that even small amounts of calcium inhibit the absorption of Zinc, hence just avoid any calcium supplements during the time frame of 2 hours before and half an hour after taking ZMA. However, because ZMA is an expensive supplement as most fitness supplements are, I personally do not want to take any chances. I avoid dairy or acidic products around the time when I take ZMA. It is even recommended to take ZMA at least two hours after any meal and half an hour before taking any other supplements. This is why I take ZMA one hour before sleep. This gives me a chance to take Casein protein powder half an hour before sleep on the days when I complete a hard bodybuilding session. Of course, ZMA can be taken on days when you do not work out, as you need the help of these testosterone and growth hormones to grow your muscles when you are recovering. I just prefer to take Casein protein powder before bed, only, if I work out hard lifting weights on that day in order to control my calories and keep my levels of body fat low to show my hard-earned six-pack.

I recommend taking ZMA before sleep so that you have a deeper sleep and your muscles grow bigger. It is during your sleep that most of muscle growth occurs. As mentioned above, avoid taking it with dairy products and take it two hours after any meal. If you do take protein powder that night, take the powder at least half an hour after taking ZMA. Some people who take ZMA ingredients separately recommend taking zinc late in the morning and magnesium late in the evening. I prefer to take it all together to avoid confusion and complications. It is difficult enough to correctly take all the various supplements at the correct times, and control your diet and exercise properly and at the right time.

RESUME

ZMA is zinc, magnesium and vitamin B6. ZMA is proved to increases natural Testosterone levels, endurance, strength, aids recovery and hydration and protects the liver. ZMA should be taken without anything acidic or containing calcium.

To save money and buy the ingredients for ZMA in a supermarket, use the following formula: 30 mg of zinc, 450 mg of magnesium and 11 mg of Vitamin B6. Take it before sleep.

ACETYL L-CARNITINE AND ALPHA LIPOIC ACID

It is also known as ALA and ALCAR. ALA stands for alpha Lipoic acid and ALCAR stands for Acetyl L-Carnitine. This supplement gained promising initial results in research labs. The results are simply unbelievable, prepare to be amazed! This supplement was fed to elderly infirmed rats. The rats were transformed in to vigorous rodents with youthful energy!

Now let me disappoint you a little bit. The downside is that this supplement has not yet been researched for a sufficient amount of time to be conclusive, nor, it was tested on humans. Some supplements work for rodents, not for humans. However, the preliminary results are so out of this world that I personally take a chance and supplement myself with it. This is another example of supplements which are not fully proven yet. Even when you visit your doctor for treatment, you find that your doctor will try many drugs on you before finding which one is the most suitable for you. Sometimes, doctors offer a trial drug that has not been fully tested yet. The combination of acetyl L-Carnitine and Alpha Lipoic acid has been already tested on humans although not to the same degree as on rodents. It has been proven on humans that it contains superior antioxidants, which fight free radicals and oxidative stress.

Alpha Lipoic acid is well known for its antioxidative properties. It is such a strong fighter of free radicals that it is used in Germany to treat nerve degeneration, resulting from Diabetes. You can trust the most diligent German approach to science. In fact, German quality control is so high that, if I had unlimited resources all of my supplements would probably come from Germany. Alpha Lipoic acid has such an effect on the nerves that even glaucoma, during which eye nerves are damaged, is treated with it. Alpha Lipoic acid is known to be therapeutic for a long list of illnesses even liver cirrhosis, which is the scaring of the liver, mostly resulting from excess alcohol consumption. However, that being said, do not totally rely on Alpha Lipoic acid because although it combats many free radicals, it does not combat all of them.

Let us consider the second, but by no means the lesser element in this supplement. Acetyl L-Carnitine has been found to increase your metabolic rate, i.e. you will burn off more calories generally, even when you are asleep. Acetyl L-Carnitine has other qualities such as it improves your cognitive function. It achieves this by increasing the nerve growth factor. To simplify, consider nerve growth factor as the same for the brain as human growth hormones and testosterone are for your muscles. Acetyl L-Carnitine also improves cognitive function by improving synaptic morphology. Morphology means structure and synaptic refers to the junctions between nerve cells. In simple words, Acetyl L-Carnitine also improves the structure of the brain. In addition to this, Acetyl L-Carnitine decreases toxic fatty acids. Do not confuse toxic fatty acids with any other fatty acids. Toxic fatty acids are trans fats (hydrogenated fats) and other fats with a toxic chemical structure for humans. Often, toxic fats differ chemically from normal fats. This, on its own is great news, because it was believed that once you had trans fats in your body you could not remove them.

If you are tempted to take one Alpha Lipoic acid but not acetyl L-Carnitine or vice versa, then do not, go the extra mile and buy a supplement combining both of them. Of course, you can still receive various benefits if you are taking one but not the other. However, in the earlier mentioned studies on rats, the effects were as if they drank a youth elixir when a combination of both was used. If you decide to buy them separately but use them together, then a usual mix is 2 parts of Acetyl L-Carnitine to 1 part of Alpha Lipoic acid. The exact mix varies because different manufacturing processes have different potencies. This is why I prefer to buy Alpha Lipoic acid and Acetyl L-Carnitine as one supplement.

I mentioned that this supplement also increases metabolism. Let us now consider this claim in more detail. Our energy is created in mitochondria. Imagine it to be like many little engines in your body. Over time as we age the engines become clogged up with sediment and become rusty due to free radicals and oxidative stresses, thus eventually these engines stop

functioning altogether. Due to the combined effort of Alpha Lipoic acid and Acetyl L-Carnitine, these engines (or mitochondria centers in our bodies) become unclogged and de-rusted which results in more mitochondria centers. The more mitochondria centers you have the more energy you have to increase your metabolism. The faster the muscle development, the faster excess fat is burnt, the leaner you are, and more muscle can be seen in a mirror e.g. the eluded six pack. This combination of Alpha Lipoic acid and Acetyl L-Carnitine is considered to be even greater as it serves as an antioxidant that even recycles the remains of other antioxidants such as Vitamins A, C and E.

How is all of the above beneficial for bodybuilding? Where do I start? In regards to improving cognitive function, you improve your brain, which is in charge of many hormones and your body. It improves all of the cell structures throughout the body including your spinal brain which controls almost every muscle in your body. Higher metabolism means a better-defined muscle physique, more energy and better muscle development. Universally, antioxidative properties mean you can work out more intensively and recover quicker. The benefits are youthful looks, better quality of life and the fact that muscle development is much easier in the younger version of you.

To conclude this chapter, let me remind you that Alpha Lipoic acid and Acetyl L-Carnitine are not just super but superior antioxidants, although they do not take care of all the free radicals, so other oxidants (e.g. vitamins) are beneficial too. Let me also remind you the study that demonstrated the youthful effect on rats. This gives a great probability, but, no certainty it would have the same effect on humans. Even then, due to other proven benefits to humans and a fantastic potential of a youth elixir, this supplement is my number 1. Do not be surprised if this supplement will become highly overpriced on the market.

RESUME

ALA and ALCAR potentially promise reinvigorated youth, but it is too early to predicate anything yet. In any case, they are more superior antioxidants than any antioxidant you can find. A bodybuilder needs to counteract the oxidative stresses gained from training. ALA even treats degenerated nerves in humans and is very beneficial for the liver. However, ALA does not cover everything and best works with ALCAR as they complement each other. ALCAR increases metabolic rate, nerve growth, improves the brain structure and decreases toxic fat. Normally, the mix is 2 parts of ALCAR to 1 part of ALA for consumption.

For a bodybuilder, an improved brain, improves hormonal production, higher metabolism results in a leaner body and better muscle development and super antioxidative properties results in a quicker recovery.

OMEGA 3, 6 AND 9

Before we discuss Omegas, it is important to realize that they are all fats. There is plenty of misconception about fats. Many people try to cut out fats altogether and this is wrong. In fact, if you take out fat from your diet, you will gain extra fat and reduce your body's ability to grow muscles. I know that many bodybuilders pay more attention when they hear anything about the muscle growing hormone testosterone. Understand this – research after research has found that testosterone levels have significantly fallen in athletes on low fat diets and testosterone levels are the highest amongst athletes who have a diet which includes plenty of healthy fats derived from eggs, dairy products, various meats, avocados, hemp, flax seeds, nuts, canola oil, olive oil and many more. The precursors to testosterone are made out of these fats, hence, if you cut fat out of your diet, you will reduce your body's production of testosterone - no fat results in no testosterone. Think again, next time when on a healthy diet. However, it does not mean that you can now eat lots of fat. Of course, if your diet is unhealthy, you definitely need to cut the fat down and eat healthy fat only in the range of recommended daily dosages. If you eat too much fat, your bad cholesterol levels will spike up resulting in heart attacks and strokes. It will increase the risk of various heart and artery diseases. There is more research confirming that Omega 3, Omega 6 and Omega 9 are crucial for many of your body processes improving your heart, making your muscle cell

membranes stronger. These fats even reduce low density cholesterol (bad cholesterol) which causes heart attacks and brain strokes by blocking the blood vessels in your body.

All of the three Omegas are types of unsaturated, monosaturated and polyunsaturated fatty acids. These fatty acids are available in animal fats, oils, nuts and seeds.

Omega 9 contains Oleic and Erucic acids. Quality Oleic fatty acid is found in olive oil and some other monosaturated fats. Erucic fatty acid can be found in good quantities of rapeseed, wallflower and mustard seed. The full list of fatty acids which Omega 9 contains is Oleic, Elaidic, Gondoic, Mead, Erucic and Nervonic acids. Omega 9 is the only one out of three omega fats that can be produced by your body. Omega 9 fats support good high density cholesterol. The cells' surfaces consist of high density cholesterol. When you have plenty of good cholesterol you fortify your muscle cells' surfaces, so they do not leek out. It is important to not confuse it with bad cholesterol – low density cholesterol – which causes blood blockages leading to heart attacks and strokes. Omega 9 also promotes the healthy production of glucose, which is energy for your workouts.

Omega 6 polyunsaturated fatty acid cannot be produced by your body and has to be gained from animal and vegetable fats or supplemented for optimal health. Omega 6 is also known as CLA – Conjugated Linoleic Acid - but it is not exactly true because Omega 6 is a category of fatty acids and some of them are Gamma Linoleic and Arachidonic acids. Omega 6 is beneficial for building muscles or burning off fat. It boosts your metabolic rate, so you burn fat and your muscles grow faster. Omega 6 helps the brain and improves the health of the nervous system. It improves your heart so that your body can deliver more blood to your muscles to feed them during a workout or when recovering. Omega 6 also helps to maintain healthy bones. The healthier bones you have the more safe you are in a gym and the healthier your blood, this is because blood cells are produced in the bones.

In the developed world, 95% of people have Omega 3 deficiency; it makes great sense to supplement with it. Your body cannot produce Omega 3 fatty acids, hence it is called essential. You must get it from a diet or supplement with it. Omega 3 is a polyunsaturated acid and is known for EPA (Eicosapen Taenoic Acid) and DHA (Docosahexaenoic Acid). Both acids are responsible for variety of health benefits. However, the same as other Omegas, Omega 3 is not a particular substance but a whole class of oils. The full list is as follows: Hexadecatrienoic acid (HTA), α-Linolenic acid (ALA), Stearidonic acid (SDA), Eicosatrienoic acid (ETE), Eicosatetraenoic acid (ETA), Eicosapentaenoic acid (EPA), Heneicosapentaenoic acid (HPA), Docosapentaenoic acid (DPA) aka Clupanodonic acid,

Docosahexaenoic acid (DHA), Tetracosapentaenoic acid, Tetracosahexaenoic acid (Nisinic acid). Do not become confused, as you do not have to remember all those names but be assured, due to the pure quantity of them, there are plenty of supplement companies insisting they have a new research and their exact mix is the best.

It is well known that fish is a particularly good source of Omega 3. Considering that prices of good quality fish are on the rise and sea fish is not easily available in many parts of the world, supplementing is highly recommended. It is also highly recommended because Western diets are particularly low in Omega 3. Omega 3 is also available in some seeds, nuts and fruits e.g. kiwi, walnuts, flax seed, lamb, tuna, salmon, hemp etc. Omega 3 the same as other Omegas promotes a healthy heart, brain and nervous system.

Now, you know about Omegas 3, 6 and 9. Does it mean you can just take any of them you like without others? The answer is not exactly. In order for any of these Omegas to be fully operational and properly absorbed, you have to consume all three of them in a particular proportion, however, depending on your diet (especially western fast food diets) you already have plenty of Omegas 6 and 9, but it is not the rule for everyone in the World. If you completely exclude fat from your diet and buy some of the very expensive Omega 3, then you might be wasting your money.

No matter how great that supplement is, Omega 3 fats still need Omega 6 and Omega 9 to be absorbed and function effectively, not everyone has the same diet.

Now let us put it in simple words: Omega 9 can be made from Omega 6 in your body, Omega 6 must be gained from a diet or as a supplement, Omega 6 might be plentiful in some unhealthy Western diets, but it does not mean you are on that diet. Both Omega 6 and 9 are required for Omega 3 to operate well. It is difficult to give exact proportions because everyone on the planet has different diets, hence, in this case, buying from your local supplements store might be a good idea because they probably cater for the locals.

The safe dose for Omega 3 is considered to be 3 grams a day (more often referred as 3000 mg) although the effects can be felt from taking 500 to 1000 mg. However, the dosages for Omega 3 and 6 are not established because it can be wildly influenced by the diet. The general advice is to avoid dosages of Omega 6 or Omega 9 of more than 3 grams per day.

These fats are essential for maintaining the nervous system which needs to work effectively, if you want to have a great workout. You may ask how so? Well, all of our effort in the gym is dependent on how well your nervous system performs. For example, when you contract one of your biceps,

motor neurons fire out your spinal cord into your bicep. The muscle itself consists of many muscle fibers, and every motor neuron is connected to a block of these muscle fibers. This whole structure is called a Motor Neuron Unit. Each muscle has a different amount of muscle fibers per one neuron e.g. your hand muscles will have less muscle fibers per neuron to manage delicate moves and your leg muscles will have more muscle fibers per neuron to deliver more powerful rather than delicate contractions. Not every motor unit can be half activated; it does it either fully or not at all. It is known as the All or Nothing Principle. Motor units, for example, in a bicep fire off for contraction interchangeably, so while some contracted fully others are resting. Now, you have an idea about this intricate interplay on Motor Neuron Units, which helps to realize how essential your nervous system is for a good workout. Now, you fully understand why supplementing with number one supplements for brain and nervous system is so important for a bodybuilder.

Omega fatty acids are essential for your muscles' cells because your cells membranes are formed of High Density Cholesterol i.e. Good Fatty Acids. Healthy membrane means that your muscle cells will gain the nutrients from your blood and will easily dispose of any waste products.

Another pronounced benefit of omegas is its role in supporting healthy joints. Again, this is crucial for a bodybuilder who wants to stay injury-free.

You are under an abnormal amount of physical stress, so you have to give your body a chance to protect itself. If your joints are painful, it is a sign to stop because if you injure yourself in some cases you can forever forget about bodybuilding.

On a Western diet, we do not need to supplement with Omega 6 or 9 because Omega 6 is abundant in all oils and meat fats. The body itself, on the other hand, can produce Omega 9. The only Omega that is rare is number 3 because fish is expensive and we do not get enough of it in Western diets.

Another point worth mentioning is that while buying Omega 3 supplements do not be conned into "cheapness". Look at the label and see how many milligrams of actual Omega 3 they contain. Sometimes, it can be as low as 250 mg per 1000 mg Omega 3 capsule. At the same time, EPA and DHA types of Omega 3 oils are the most scientifically proven, hence they are more expensive. Next time, you are buying Omega 3 oils pay attention. Compare and observe that the more expensive Omega 3 supplement has the largest amount of EPA and DHA Omega 3 type oils. If you do your calculation properly, you will discover that the more expensive a supplement is, the higher the quality of the oil. If the supplement does not provide you with the actual type of Omega 3 oils it contains, be aware, it seems to be an inferior product hiding behind an expensive brand.

Above all, Omegas are great for a healthy heart. Your heart can efficiently pump blood and your muscle will receive more oxygen and nutrients, therefore you can train harder and then repair and grow your muscles.

RESUME

Good fats are essential for the body. Even Testosterone levels drop with low fat diets. Omega 3, Omega 6 and Omega 9 improve your heart, strengthen your muscle cell membranes, reduce Bad Cholesterol and support healthy joints. Omegas are types of unsaturated, monosaturated and polyunsaturated fatty acids.

Omega 3 and Omega 6 cannot be produced by the body. Omega 9 can be produced from unsaturated fats. Modern diets are usually high in other Omegas 6 and 9 and 95% of people are deficient in Omega 3, hence it is reasonable to supplement with Omega 3 only. There are many types of Omega 3, but the well-researched and more effective omegas are EPA and DHA. The recommended dosage of Omega 3 is 3000 mg. If you prefer quality to quantity, always chose Omega 3 made of EPA and DHA.

LIVER SUPPORTING MILK THISTLE AND N-ACETYL CYSTEINE (NAC)

Milk thistle is a plant of the daisy family and is native to the Mediterranean. Research after research has proven that the seeds contain Silymarin flavonoids that regenerate and protect the liver. On the top of this, they are antioxidants.

N-Acetyl Cysteine (NAC) is water soluble of the amino acid L-Cysteine. One of the best known qualities of NAC is that it supports the immune system. Another great quality of NAC is that it converts into glutathione, thus it replenishes the stores of glutathione. Glutathione binds itself to toxins in the liver and neutralizes them.

Bodybuilders use many supplements repeatedly putting their livers under stress; hence, Milk Thistle and NAC are essential supplements. A good liver indicates a body, which is functioning properly. It absorbs all that is needed and creates an anabolic muscle-growing environment. Think about it, if your liver does not absorb properly, you are wasting money on supplements that are absorbed by the liver. Milk Thistle and NAC removes the toxins that accumulate there. Bodybuilding supplements are not perfect. Due to manufacturing processes, some toxins might remain in the supplements themselves. Also if you attend parties which involve drinking alcohol; you should consume Milk Thistle and NAC to protect your liver.

Typical dosage for Milk Thistle are 200 mg 1 to 3 times a day; it does not matter when your take it. For the very best results, Milk Thistle is used in conjunction with N-Acetyl Cysteine (NAC). The usual dosage for N-Acetyl Cysteine (NAC) is 600 mg per day.

RESUME

The liver is compromised with the consumption of many bodybuilding supplements. The liver absorbs nutrients and a healthy liver means the supplements are properly transferred into your body. To take care of the liver, take Milk Thistle 200 mg 1 to 3 times a day and N-Acetyl Cysteine (NAC) 600 mg per day.

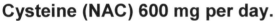

EXTRACT OF GINKGO BILOBA

The Ginkgo Biloba herb comes from a tree that can live for over 1000 years. It is a very powerful antioxidant. During intense exercise, Cortisol is produced as a result. Cortisol is the nemesis of every bodybuilder it makes your body break down muscles to fuel your body, thus it drives your body into a Catabolic State. A state during which your hard-earned muscles are eaten by your body. One study has demonstrated that the Extract of Ginkgo Biloba decreases the levels of Cortisol. Do not confuse the Extract of Ginkgo Biloba with anything else; it is not the same as a Ginkgo supplement many stores sell. It is the Extract of Ginkgo Biloba, which was specifically researched. Regarding reducing Cortisol, it is worth knowing that dehydration is even worse when Cortisol levels increase. Dehydration slows down the speed of delivery of essential nutrients in your body, so drink plenty of water.

Ginkgo is useful for the whole of your body. It dilates your blood vessels, thus more nutrients, including oxygen, are delivered to your muscles, brain, eyes, ears, arms, legs, etc. Ginkgo is also a very powerful antioxidant. Antioxidants as mentioned previously are elements with an extra electron on the orbit. This can be given away to another damaged element for repair. Free radicals are the opposite. They have an incomplete set of electrons on its orbit, so it scavenges your body to gain a full set. In simple words, free radicals are ripping all of your cells including your muscles apart and antioxidants fight them. The Extract of Ginkgo Biloba not only improves your muscle cells, but also helps you have clearer thoughts. Ginkgo is even known to correct the eyesight and hearing.

Ginkgo is taken from 40 mg to 240 mg over a day. It has no known toxicity issues, so overdose is unlikely.

So what is the conclusion of this miracle antioxidant, which lowers Cortisol levels that breaks down your muscles for energy? Well, in spite of all the science behind it, I am not convinced. It is an expensive supplement that can be beneficial, but is not high on the priority list of a bodybuilder. Yes, it is an antioxidant and it dilates you blood vessels, but, realistically, not everyone is going to fork out tons of cash every month on every supplement. Priority is the key here. However, if you want to take it, can afford it and are prepared to be meticulous about taking hundreds of different supplements a day, then Ginkgo is a good herb that is proven beneficial. One thing though, only take Extract of Ginkgo Biloba and not any other form. Only consume the forms that have been researched.

RESUME

Ginkgo Biloba is a herb and a very powerful antioxidant. Ginkgo decrease Cortisol levels, dilates blood vessels and helps clearer thoughts. It is the extract of Ginkgo Biloba that has been researched so buy the extract, not anything with Ginkgo on it.

Take 40 mg to 240 mg distributed over a day. However, it is not on a bodybuilder's priority list.

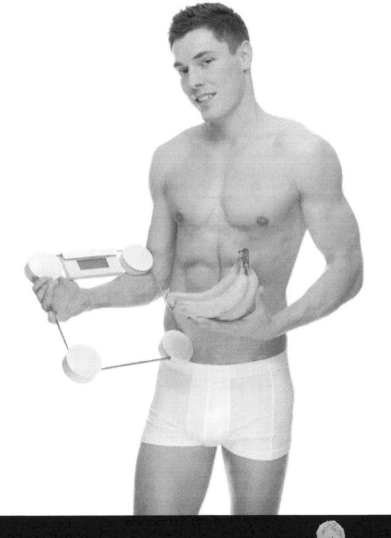

GABA

Gamma Amino Butyric Acid (GABA) was discovered in 1883 in Berlin, in the body it is produced from Glutamine. GABA is a neurotransmitter, which is produced in the brain from glutamine. GABA as a supplement is available in tomatoes plentifully. Neurotransmitters are special chemicals in your body, which transmit signals from your nerves to your cells; in our case, to your muscle cells. There are several varieties of neurotransmitters. GABA is one of the main ones, which is responsible for the tone of the muscle. Do not confuse GABA with other amino acids that you supplement with for muscle nutrition. They are different. The other amino acids, which we discussed in this book, are incorporated into proteins, not like GABA.

Study after study demonstrates that GABA increases the production of the Human Growth Hormone. Some studies claim to have found results with an increase of 650% in Human Growth Hormone. The more you have of the Human Growth, the greater benefit for your muscles as your muscles need it for growth. Human Growth Hormone is also responsible for metabolism in your body. As we grow older, we receive less and less of it. It is partly due to this that, as we grow, it is harder to lose fat.

GABA also promotes good sleep, which leads to better muscle recovery. It does so because it is a very good neurotransmitter. It also reduces pain

and is even prescribed as an anti-depressant in some countries. If you have a very intense lifestyle or are stressed, it might be a good idea to take GABA. At the moment, it is relatively cheaper than other partially proven remedies. GABA is so established and effective, that in Russia, it is often used as an antidepressant. Since the era of the Soviet Union, Russia has won the majority of the Olympic gold medals and it is very competitive with the United States since the Soviet times.

The usual dosage for GABA is 3 to 5 grams a day. It does make sense to take it before sleep due to its calming qualities. If you are taking ZMA before sleep, feel free to add GABA; there are not any known incompatibilities between these two supplements. However, some research states that GABA may inhibit other amino acids, so it is better to take GABA separately from proteins and amino acids. Be warned that GABA can result in itchy sensations, similar to Beta Alanine. Some people get a shortness of breath. Both of these side effects are common to GABA.

RESUME

GABA is a neurotransmitter produced in the body from Glutamine. GABA is plentiful in tomatoes. GABA increases the production of Human Growth Hormones and promotes deep sleep, so that the muscles can recover.

The usual dosage is 3 to 5 grams a day and it is best taken before sleep.

POTASSIUM, SODIUM AND OTHER BODYBUILDERS' MINERALS

Potassium and Sodium are minerals that we consume in our diets. You are right to say that Sodium is common salt. Many health conscious people shout about cutting salt out of our diet, but read on and see why the bodybuilders' needs are different to everyone else's. A good balance of Potassium and Sodium is crucial for a bodybuilder because they are the biggest two minerals responsible for rehydration and protein synthesis. Before considering Potassium and Sodium together, let us consider Potassium's specific properties as Potassium does have some very distinct properties from Sodium.

Potassium is sometimes referred as vitamin K that is not true because it is a mineral. The confusion comes from the fact that Potassium is marked with K on the chemical periodic table. Vitamin K is a completely different nutrient; do not confuse it with Potassium.

Potassium is found in many foods e.g. bananas, vegetables, tomatoes, citrus fruits, milk, beans, watermelon etc. Supplement with Potassium if you are on a low carbohydrate diet because, in most cases, it means you have low levels of Potassium. Be aware, if you take multivitamins. They may already contain Potassium.

Potassium is great especially for a workout or intense activity. Potassium is an essential mineral for your nervous system, which is responsible for the brain, clarity of thoughts and proper muscle contractions. Potassium reduces you heart beat i.e. your heart become more efficient and pumps more blood with every beat. It also reduces your blood pressure. Your blood vessels widened, so that the blood easily flows to your muscles to give your muscles all the nutrients for growth. Potassium also strengthens your bones which you greatly need considering that you subject your bones to huge stresses. Potassium also helps to prevent gym injuries so that your bodybuilding goals are not ruined.

Be extremely careful with Potassium. It is not just a pill you can take as much as you like. Potassium overdose can instantly kill by causing a heart attack. It does not matter if your heart is as strong as the heart of a bull. Excessive levels of Potassium can kill even those with a strong heart. It is hard to pinpoint the correct dosage for Potassium because it all depends on your diet. Fruits are very high in Potassium. If you eat your fruit and vegetable plentifully then you need to be extremely cautious during supplementation with Potassium otherwise you risk a heart attack.

Potassium and Sodium must be combined together to gain any significant benefit. Many bodybuilders are so scared by all the talk against the Sodium (aka Salt) that they eliminate it from their diets. Sodium is necessary for

your body. Of course, it has to be at the right dosage, but the required dosage is higher for bodybuilders. Because enough research has not been done into how much salt a bodybuilder needs, it is subject to theories. It is clear that a drastic reduction in salt intake is not recommended for a serious bodybuilder. Yes, of course, confirm it with you doctor etc. but do not expect them to know how much salt a bodybuilder is expected to take. Yes, high salt does cause high blood pressure; too much salt will put you at risk of a heart attack. Hence, understand what I have said and do your own research, you are the only one who is responsible for any side effects and your doctor would be the best person to ask for an advice as he knows your health history.

Bodybuilders can become dehydrated regularly and severely, if they do not rehydrate themselves properly. Even slight dehydration affects your effort in the gym and significantly slows down any muscle growth. If you drink water to rehydrate, it is not the most effective way. Expensive sports drinks contain Potassium and Sodium to rehydrate. It is not exactly water that must be replaced while sweating in a gym; it is electrolytes that need to be replaced. Potassium constitutes a major part of these electrolytes.

Potassium and Sodium make up most of the minerals in the body. They are important in balancing body water. Although it is important to maintain the individual levels of minerals, but the overall balance of these minerals is more important. Other minerals like Magnesium and Calcium are also important, thus it is a good idea to take multivitamins containing all the minerals.

Sodium is involved in extracellular water balance while Potassium is involved in intracellular water balance. Normally, we have more water inside our cells. Around 60% of our body's water is in the cells in normal conditions. This balance should be more or less maintained for us to function optimally. With Sodium and Potassium in your diet, you cover the outsides and insides of the cells. Water does not flow into your cells by itself; instead, water follows the solutes such as Sodium and Potassium. If you want to hydrate your muscles' cells, Potassium is not enough. A correct balance should be between Potassium and Sodium.

It is ultimately the kidneys, which influence your water balance. As soon as you decide to cut out salt (Sodium) from your diet, your body will respond by increasing a hormone called Aldosterone. Then the kidneys will react to Aldosterone and respond by preserving Sodium in your body. Sodium will be prevented from being absorbed into your blood i.e. water will not completely enter your blood. Just after a week on a low Sodium diet, your Sodium content in the blood reduces to one tenth of the original amount.

As you now understand, the kidneys respond to the increase of Aldosterone, which, in turn, decreases Sodium in the blood. It is also important to remember that if you take too much Potassium, the production of Aldosterone hormone is also increased which causes Sodium to decrease in the blood. Thus, it is crucial to have Potassium in the correct dosages. The best way to stay rehydrated is to have a good diet with a moderate amount of salt and plenty of Potassium (greens, fruits and vegetables). If you have low amounts of Sodium in your blood, your muscle cells will leak water. In other words, they will deflate and you muscles will shrink.

In fact, the most efficient way to keep your body hydrated through minerals is to take multivitamins containing multiminerals.

Potassium's special quality is its ability to decrease muscle soreness, hence you can recover faster and be more efficient during your next workout. Both Sodium and Potassium are essential for protein synthesis and nutrient transportation to the muscle cells. This is why they are mentioned in this bodybuilding book. A severe reduction in muscle growth is caused by the lack of Potassium and Sodium.

For Potassium, the recommended dosage is 2 grams per day. However, you must take into account the Potassium from your diet. For Sodium, the recommended daily intake for a bodybuilder is 2 to 3 grams a day. 3 grams is considered too high for someone who does not take part in sweat breaking activities on a regular basis. However, it is not worth supplementing with Sodium because in most cases no matter where you are on the planet you get plenty of it from modern diets. It is not suitable to consume too much or too little salt. Do not consume too much of it or you will risk high blood pressure and heart attacks. Do not cut it out altogether, if you are a bodybuilder, because it is an important element which supports optimal muscle hydration and nutrient transportation.

To conclude, the best solution is multiminerals' supplementation. Beyond hydration, a multiminerals cocktail for a bodybuilder would have to have minerals that are directly involved in muscle action and growth, protein synthesis and improving performance. Sometimes, intense physical activity demands higher amounts of specific minerals. The list of essential minerals for a bodybuilder is as follows:

- Potassium as discussed in this chapter
- Sodium as discussed in this chapter
- Copper, which increases blood flow during a strenuous workout and transports oxygen to create energy.
- Iron, which also transports oxygen and, is responsible for Hemoglobin - the main mode of transport for oxygen in red blood cells. Thus, your

recovery between sets is shortened if your blood contains more red blood cells.

- Phosphorus is directly involved in the production of ATP – Adenosine TriPhosphate. If you have read the book so far, you know that ATP is the principal fuel for bodybuilders during weightlifting. Phosphorus works in conjunction with Calcium. When both are supplemented, the proportion of Phosphorus to Calcium is 1:1. This proportion is very important because the system will not work effectively, if it is incorrect. One of the benefits of Phosphorus is its ability to reduce the acidity of muscles during a workout – acidity causes muscle fatigue.

- Calcium is one of the most important substances because, although it is one of the most abundant minerals in the body, frequently, it is not consumed in the right proportion with Phosphorus. Bodybuilders have very high protein diets, which contain plenty of Phosphorus. If a bodybuilder for one reason or another does not have as much Calcium as Phosphorus (in proportion 1:1), they might experience Calcium deficiency. Calcium is also vital for bodybuilders because it is a prime mineral involved in the proper contractions of muscle at the micro level of individual muscle fibers. Further, Calcium is important to maintain bone density and avoid injuries. Remember that it is crucial to supplement yourself with Vitamin D as it helps Calcium to be absorbed. On the plus side, Vitamin D also is known to improve your mood during winter when the sun is not bright.

- Magnesium is often thought to be the most important mineral for a bodybuilder because of its potent involvement in energy production and protein synthesis. Magnesium is especially important for bodybuilders because sweating indicates that you are working out properly, but, through sweating, you lose excessive amounts of Magnesium, which must be replaced. To complicate the situation further, a typical bodybuilder's diet does not contain enough Magnesium such as nuts. Several researches were conducted to test the increase in the performance of weightlifting through Magnesium supplementation.

- Zinc is critical for any kind of muscle growth; no zinc means no growth, and bodybuilders while working out hard lose huge quantities of it, thus Zinc is an essential mineral for supplementation.

- Chromium helps Insulin to transport amino acids, fatty acids and glucose into the muscle cells. Chromium is known as an element, which increases Insulin sensitivity. With higher sensitivity, more muscle cells respond to Insulin to accept the nutrients it carries.

- Vanadium, although not very well researched, theoretically, is the mineral that helps to increase the Glycogen stores in your muscles. In simple words, it helps your muscles to store more energy and replenish Glycogen stores so that you recover faster. However, I am not in a rush to buy it because further research is needed. It is mentioned in this book because it is discussed frequently in the bodybuilding community.

Truth about Bodybuilding Supplements

Only for Professional Bodybuilders

To conclude, have a healthy diet. Having a healthy diet does not mean avoiding Sodium. The best way to supplement with minerals for bodybuilding is to take a good multimineral supplement.

RESUME

Potassium and Sodium are the main two minerals crucial for rehydration and protein synthesis.

Potassium is abundant in fruits and vegetable. Those who are on Carbohydrates restricted diet should consider supplementing with Potassium. Potassium decreases muscle soreness, widens the blood vessels and improves blood circulation. Potassium overdose can be fatal, be careful. 3 grams per day including that from your diet is the recommended dose for an active bodybuilder.

Sodium (salt) is plentiful in the modern diet; many cut out Sodium completely. Generally, this is not advised for an active bodybuilder.

Both Sodium and Potassium are essential for hydration. Sodium controls extracellular hydration whilst Potassium controls intracellular hydration.

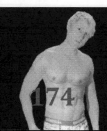

Truth about Bodybuilding Supplements
Only for Professional Bodybuilders

However, many other minerals are recommended for protein synthesis and hydration. The best way forward is to take overall multimineral supplements. The bodybuilders' minerals list is as follows:

- Potassium
- Sodium
- Copper for blood flow and oxygen transport
- Iron for oxygen transport
- Phosphorus for energy production
- Calcium for muscle contractions, healthy bones and balance with Phosphorus
- Magnesium for energy production and protein synthesis
- Zinc for muscle growth
- Chromium for transporting nutrients to muscles
- Vanadium supposedly for the replenishment of Glycogen for energy

MULTIVITAMINS, MULTIMINERALS AND SUPER GREENS

This is not really a book on Vitamins and minerals; however, it is worth mentioning them because they can be used effectively in bodybuilding.

If your workouts are hard and you visit the gym regularly, it is a great idea to supplement yourself with vitamins and minerals. As we discussed, the molecules that are used for the muscles' energy are called ATP (refer to the chapter on Creatine). ATP is the principal energy source of your body. When you train hard, your cells predominately produce ATP energy using oxygen. Later, this oxygen is converted into water, however, in the process, so-called Reactive Oxygen is created as a by-product. Reactive Oxygen is a free radical, which tears apart other cells. In this instance, it opens the surface of the muscle cells. Calcium floods into these muscle cells, which in turn activates the breakdown of the muscle cells. In normal circumstances, your body has enough anti-oxidants (anti free radicals in essence) to counteract these free radicals. During a workout, your heart rate increases and your consumption of oxygen rockets which results in unabated amounts of Reactive Oxygen. This degenerates your muscles. This particular effect on your muscle is called Oxidative Stress. To combat the Oxidative stress, antioxidative multivitamin supplements are recommended. Vitamin E and B9 (also known as Folic acid) are particularly good at combating Oxidative Stress. In one study, Vitamin B9 was found to be 20

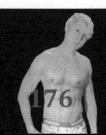

times more efficient than Vitamin C. Still Vitamin C is also useful as it is an antioxidant and, is more useful for other purposes. Some bodybuilders take a large dose of vitamin C before a workout, as it is an antioxidant, which is known to reduce your heart rate. A lower heart rate results indicates a more efficient body, thus you can exercise more correctly. Additionally, because it is very hard to overdose on Vitamins C or B, they can be taken in mega doses as the excess is removed as urine. It is especially convenient to use dissolvable Vitamins as you can dissolve them in water, which you can drink during a workout.

B Vitamins might be a little less effective in reducing oxidative stress than other vitamins. However, B Vitamins are the most recognized vitamins for bodybuilders. This is because they are key in converting Carbohydrates and fat into energy. Deficiency in B Vitamins is accompanied by low energy, low motivation and no muscle growth. It is believed that the most important B Vitamins are B1 (Thiamine), B2 (Riboflavin), B3 (Niacin), B5 (Pantothenic Acid), B6 (Pyridoxine), B7 (Biotin), B9 (Folic Acid) and B12 (Cobalamin).

These particular examples of the fight against Oxidative Stress and lower heart rate for more productive workouts demonstrates certain effects of multivitamins. A whole encyclopedia can be written on the benefits of various multivitamins; however, it is not sensible write all the benefits in one book. In simple terms, take your multivitamins. Chose those multivitamins which also contain multiminerals or buy multiminerals separately because, normally, the dosages of minerals in All in One multi vitamins and minerals are very low. The idea is simple. Even those who do not train need vitamin and mineral supplementation for good health. Additionally, some minerals are great for hydration, other minerals like Zinc and Magnesium aid Testosterone production, Potassium helps hydration, Calcium help proper muscle function, Iron enriches the blood and is good for sustained energy etc. Many minerals are discussed throughout the book and it is not really an encyclopedia on health supplements. This book is about bodybuilding supplements. Many of the reputable multiminerals and multivitamins supplements already contain all you need, according to the latest research.

It is worth mentioning about vitamin and mineral dosages. It is somewhat a very controversial issue. A large body of research demonstrates that super high strength multi vitamins and minerals are found to be more effective than standard strength ones from the shelves of most supermarkets. Even a few protests occurred when governmental bodies tried to ban high strength vitamins and minerals because of health and safety issues. It is hard to call this one. Personally, I am convinced that high strength vitamins and minerals are for high intensity bodybuilders. Bodybuilders have extraordinary needs, thus they need more than a coach potato. However, it is your personal choice and only you can take responsibility about what you

put in your mouth. If unsure, consult your doctor. You also have to know that some vitamins and minerals can have side effects and be toxic when overdosed.

As mentioned before vitamins and minerals are really classed as health supplements rather than bodybuilding supplements. Most of the vitamins, especially relevant to bodybuilding, have already been mentioned in this chapter. There are only a couple more left that a bodybuilder should know. It is a good idea to make sure you supplement with Vitamin D, which is crucial for absorbing Calcium for healthy bones. Recent research on Vitamin D has also found that it might increase Testosterone levels, which is a key for muscle growth. Vitamin D is also known to improve your mood and immune system. Another recent research has found the benefits of the so called Vitamin K. Vitamin K1 is for bones' health and blood clotting and Vitamin K2 is to increase Testosterone production.

Another fantastic alternative or addition to multi vitamins and minerals are Super Greens supplements. Super Greens are supplements which contain extracts from grasses like wheatgrass, seaweed etc. They are fantastic for your body as they contain most of the vitamins and minerals that you need. Additionally, Super Greens also contain almost all of the amino acids and loads of enzymes. Super Greens do not only have the enzymes, but they also stimulate the body's own enzymes. Enzymes are elements that help other nutrients to convert from one form to another. Without enzymes, chemical reactions would take place in the body. All bodybuilding supplements require enzymes to be digested and further transformed.

Before we move on to another chapter, it is worth mentioning that some Vitamins and minerals suppress other Vitamins and minerals. The chemistry is so complex that you would need a degree to understand it. To address this issue, the best multivitamins and multiminerals are sold in separate capsules to be taken separately at different times of the day. Some Vitamins and minerals supplements have a so-called time-release formula that addresses this issue. Of course, the price tag of these supplements is significant because it is a high end product with super strength and an optimized delivery method. It is also important to remember that most multivitamins do not have high enough dosage for a bodybuilder. These Vitamins are B Vitamins, Vitamin C (Ascorbic Acid), Vitamin D, Vitamin E and K Vitamins, so do look out for super strength Vitamins if you are a bodybuilder who visits a gym and works intensely.

RESUME

A bodybuilder because of the intense oxidative stress from working out and the need for hydration requires vitamins and minerals. Additionally, vitamins and minerals aid muscle growth. Vitamins also require minerals to be absorbed. Some evidence shows that mega multivitamins and minerals are the most efficient, however, consult your doctor because some governments were banning high dosage vitamins and minerals.

A great alternative or addition to multivitamins and minerals are Super Greens supplement which contain vitamins and minerals plus enzymes.

NITRIC OXIDE BOOSTERS

Nitric Oxide boosters are the supplements, which increase blood flow to the muscles by dilating blood or widening the blood vessels. Of course, blood transports all the nutrients and Oxygen around the body. Specifically, in regards to muscles, a high amount of supplied nutrients and Oxygen means you can lift more, workout harder and recover quicker. Arginine, Beta Alanine and Citrulline are amino acid based Nitric Oxide boosters (NO boosters). Please read the relevant chapters on these amino acids to understand their specific benefits and how to use them. When most bodybuilders say "Nitric Oxide", they refer to L-Arginine amino acid, which is converted in to Nitric Oxide in your body. What is this Nitric Oxide? Well, it is one of the most essential elements for muscle growth. In fact, many non-Testosterone steroids increase the Nitric Oxide balance in your muscles. These steroids are called anabolic steroids and are as popular as Testosterone itself. A positive Nitric Oxide balance means that your body has switched off from a Catabolic mode (during which your muscles can be burnt for energy) to an Anabolic mode (during which your muscle mass grows). Nitric Oxide is proven to improve the efficiency of Oxygen in the body by 11%, which leads to a 20% increase in the intensity of a workout.

L-Arginine and other proteins are not the only source of Nitric Oxide Boosters. Fruits and vegetables also contain high levels of Nitric Oxide.

The most fitting example is beetroot which is naturally abundant in Nitric Oxide. It is interesting to see how in the past beetroot juice was cheap and, as soon as research about Nitric Oxide dawned on the bodybuilding community, the prices increased several fold.

However, the definition of Nitric Oxide Boosters does not limit it to the elements out of which Nitric Oxide is made; anything that promotes Nitric Oxide is a NO Booster. Garlic is one of them because it dilates your blood easing the nutrient flow to your muscles, which promotes positive NO Muscle Balance. Alpha Lipoic Acid also promotes positive NO Muscle Balance and it is one of the most promising supplements on the market because of its other fantastic properties. In fact, anything that dilates blood and improves circulation can be classed as a Nitric Oxide Booster.

The other class of Nitric Oxide Boosters like beetroot concentrate are also antioxidants. Understand that Nitric Oxide only lasts for a few seconds in your muscles, Nitric Oxide stays active for longer, if more antioxidants are available.

If we consider the most popular Nitric Oxide Boosters, they will be:

1.   L-Arginine and its forms
2.   Agmatine
3.   Citrulline
4.   Beetroot Based

If your goal is to increase your overall performance during a workout by taking it 30 minutes before a workout, all of them are good. If you want a natural drink to hydrate yourself during a workout session, beetroot can be a good choice. It has the benefits of promoting Nitric Balance by providing powerful Vitamin antioxidants. It can also provide Potassium and Sodium salts, which are necessary during intensive activities. The beetroot effects will last for a maximum of 90 minutes.

However, your goal might be to promote a general Nitric Oxide balance to open up your muscles and kick them into a state of anabolic muscle growth. Of course, you would think the best time to increase your Nitric Oxide balance is during your sleep; hence you would take a Nitric Oxide supplement before sleep. Well, in this case, supplementing with L-Arginine can be a seriously bad idea, although you might be recovering after a strenuous workout, you are not in a strenuous workout. You are resting and recovering, and any extra L-Arginine, instead of being consumed immediately on the spot, will react with the body in such a way that the

body will down regulate the natural production of Arginine. Eventually, you might inhibit endogenous Arginine production altogether. This is why I prefer to use Citrulline before sleep to L-Arginine.

RESUME

Nitric Oxide boosters are the supplements which increase blood flow to the muscles by dilating the blood or widening the blood vessels. Nitric Oxide boosters are some of the most essential elements for muscle growth. In fact, many non-Testosterone steroids increase the Nitric Oxide balance in your muscles. These steroids are called anabolic steroids and are as popular as Testosterone itself as a better Nitric Oxide balance promotes muscle growth.

The most common NO boosters are:
- **L-Arginine and its forms**
- **Agmatine**
- **Citrulline**
- **Beetroot Based**

All of them are great for supplementing during a workout. Citrulline is also recommended before bed.

L-ARGININE, HCL, AKG, KIC, ETHYL ESTER

Arginine is known as a conditionally essential amino acid. Your body can produce it and, normally, you are not required to supplement with it. You only need to supplement with it when your body goes through great physical stresses during a workout. Arginine is present in nuts and seeds (especially almonds and peanuts). In the body, Arginine is also synthesized from Citrulline. Citrulline, as a supplement, is a winner in comparison to Arginine. Arginine is one of the main Nitric Oxide boosters, which expands your arteries and veins to deliver more blood with nutrients and paramount oxygen into your muscles. It also buffers the fatigue of the muscles. Another benefit of Arginine is that, in higher dosages, it increases Insulin levels which aids further nutrient transportation to the muscles. Additionally to these benefits for bodybuilders, Arginine improves the immune system. Some writers become overexcited or over motivated by selling it. Then they claim that it is essential for the production of hormones especially the Human Growth Hormone etc. In reply, I state that water is also essential, but you do not load up with it to increase your Testosterone or Human Growth Hormones. We always have to look at its significant impact and not its participation in bodily processes. I repeat again because it is crucial – Always question the significant impact of the supplement and not its participation in bodily processes. If it does not have a significant impact, it is not worth buying it. Gain it from a diet instead.

There several types of Arginine which are manufactured differently and they are very similar to manufactured protein types:

1.   L-Arginine - This is the most common form. I would trust it the most because other formulas tend to be too fragile to pass through the liver and stomach. Besides, the higher price for a slightly different formula is unreasonable when the original formula gives a positive result at a cheaper price. It might be sensible to use other forms, for some reason, you do not feel any effect from Arginine in its simple form.

2.   L-Arginine HCL (Arginine Hydrochloride) - Arginine is mixed with Hydrogen Chloride (Hydrochloride) to make the taste tolerable and supposedly increase absorption by your stomach.

3.   L-Arginine AKG is the combination of two nutrients– Arginine salt and Alpha KetoGlutarate (AKG). This form is thought to be more absorbent. AKG is a precursor of Glutamine, which further helps the production and maintenance of Arginine.

4.   L-Arginine KIC is the combination of two nutrients – Arginine and Alpha KetoIsoCaproate (KIC). This form is thought to be even more absorbent than L-Arginine AKG.

5.   L-Arginine Ethyl Ester, which is a form of Arginine, which supposedly helps the absorption of Arginine. Again, the issue with Ester is that it is not exactly known if this form is stable enough to transfer into blood without much degradation. Degradation starts from the storage of the supplement and as soon as you put it in your mouth.

The main benefit of Arginine, also known as L-Arginine, which is one of the amino acids, is its effect on so-called NO in your body. NO stands for Nitric Oxide, which is one atom of Nitrogen and one atom of Oxygen. Nitric Oxide increases blood flow, which is known in bodybuilding by the term Muscle Pumps. Nitric Oxide is also important for the release of Insulin from the pancreas and Insulin transports nutrients to the cells of your body. Your body creates Nitric Oxide from Arginine, thus Arginine is recommended as a supplement when you exercise hard. However, little research has been carried out on this matter. Yes, the theory is sound and widely agreed upon but it is just a theory, hence taking Arginine, as a supplement, is speculative.

Arginine has potential side effects. It thins the blood. Let us say you are already taking blood thinning pills and then Arginine further thins your blood so that your wounds cannot heal. Arginine is also not recommended to someone recovering from a heart attack or if someone has a liver or kidney disease. However, you always have to consult your doctor before taking anything, especially when you already have medical conditions and are already medicated.

I personally think that Arginine in your pre-workout protein shake should be enough. Dosages, if you do want to supplement, is up to 6 grams daily, however, 3 grams a day can be sufficient to raise NO levels. It is 3 grams a

day that has been used in many of the studies. Bodybuilders who supplement with more than 6 grams hope to gain another result of Arginine. Arginine in high dosages increases Insulin levels. Insulin transports proteins into the muscles growth. Some people take Glutamine together with Arginine because Glutamine also produces the so-called Citrulline, which in turn raises the levels of Arginine in your blood by as much as two fold. Of course, those who are interested and have plenty of spare cash will take Arginine together with Citrulline and Glutamine.

There is another important point about the suitable time to take Arginine. Yes, of course, most bodybuilders including myself use Arginine as a pre-workout solution. However, its capacity to boost Nitric Oxide is triggered during the night and not around the time of the workout. One may think that they will take it before sleep. Again, this is wrong. Because if you take Arginine twice a day, especially before sleep, you can suppress your own body's natural production of Arginine. The body can literally stop producing it; this is not what a bodybuilder wants. The answer is to use Citrulline before sleep because Citrulline is the precursor of Arginine production; hence, your body will be busy producing Arginine without being suppressed. In any case, Citrulline is my preference over Arginine.

RESUME

Arginine is only essential during a hard workout. Arginine is an amino acid, which is produced from Citrulline in the body. Citrulline as a supplement is more effective.

Arginine expands your blood vessels, delivers more blood and nutrients to the muscles, buffers muscle fatigue and increases healthy Insulin production to aid nutrient absorption by muscles.

There several types of Arginine, which vary in absorption and taste:
- L-Arginine
- L-Arginine HCL
- L-Arginine ACG
- L-Arginine KIC
- L-Arginine Ethyl Ester

In spite of the fact that NO is created form Arginine which promotes muscle growth, insufficient research has been carried out to confirm Arginine's undoubted benefits. Hence, Arginine's results are speculative now.

Truth about Bodybuilding Supplements
Only for Professional Bodybuilders

It is important to avoid over supplementing with Arginine as it can suppress the body's natural production of it. Arginine is risky for those recovering from heart attacks and liver or kidney failures. Always ask your doctor before using any of the supplements described in this book.

The recommended dosage is 3 to 6 grams a day and the best time to take it is before a workout.

AGMATINE

Agmatine is a by-product of Arginine. Yes, of course, because it is yet another new form of NO booster based on Arginine you might hear a lot of excitement about it. This is mainly because of marketing by the supplement companies. The marketing of Agmatine normally states it has more potential than Arginine itself. I doubt it, because Arginine is very poorly researched. Now, they have developed a derivative from Arginine and applied plenty of marketing, but if you try it and it works for you, it is great. The point here is that not enough research has been done to understand most supplements. Additionally, hundreds of different forms of the same supplement have not been researched properly or researched at all. May be this is beneficial to the supplement companies. They want more people to believe them so that they can gain a larger profit. May be the sporting and governmental bodies have done research on many of the fitness supplements, but they will not disclose the research because it is their secret in winning the Olympics etc.

Let us just have a quick look through the claims. Please keep in mind that the same benefits might be achieved through Arginine out of which Agmatine is made. Agmatine might lower high blood pressure (any blood thinners do that). It is a neurotransmitter which can improve your mental focus during exercise. It is an antioxidant for fighting free radicals. It might

aid kidney function (I would not trust this claim because Arginine is suspected to do the opposite). It stimulates Calcium uptake. It is claimed to have antidepressant qualities. It is a painkiller and improves insulin production (insulin transports nutrients to the muscles).

All of the above-mentioned qualities are in addition to the fact that it is an NO booster, which delays muscle fatigue and aids recovery.

However, there is really no point in describing Agmatine further because its benefits are the same as the benefits of Arginine. If you have not read the chapter on Arginine, it is recommended to read it now.

After my research, I have concluded that for all the promises and claimed benefits it is not worth the premium price in comparison to the simple Arginine. However, if this suits your body, you can use it. Agmatine is normally taken 30 to 60 minutes before a workout at a dosage of 500 to 1000 mg.

RESUME

Agmatine is a by-product of Arginine and some claim it is more potent, however Arginine itself is not well researched and the derivative Agmatine has hardly been researched. The claims are that Agmatine lowers blood pressure, thins blood for nutrient transport, improves mental focus and insulin production, delays fatigue and speed up muscle recovery.

Agmatine is a premium product with a premium price, but if you want this form of Arginine which is the most suitable for you and your stomach, dosages of 500 mg to 1000 mg 30 to 60 minutes before a workout are recommended.

CITRULLINE

Citrulline is an Alpha Amino Acid and is produced from Ornithine and Carbamoyl Phosphate. A few preliminary studies have discovered that Citrulline can improve cardio and weightlifting. One research states that Citrulline increases the number of bench press reps by as much as 50%. Citrulline is found to improve the use of Creatine and various amino acids, which are muscle building blocks. Citrulline also increases the levels of Bicarbonate, which buffers the muscles' fatigue because it reduces acidity in the muscles (excess acidity causes the onset of fatigue). Citrulline also, similar to Arginine, increases Nitric Oxide levels which further buffers muscle acidity. Citrulline also increases Arginine production to further buffer muscle fatigue. One of the most exciting benefits of Citrulline is that it increases the availability of Nitrogen, which triggers anabolic muscle growing. Some people take steroids to achieve the availability of Nitrogen.

An advantage of Citrulline is that your liver and stomach do not affect it. Citrulline is directly absorbed into your blood without being broken down by the stomach or liver.

If I had to chose between Arginine and Citrulline, Citrulline is the winner hands downs because more research has been done on it (although on

rats and not humans). Additionally, it has more benefits and, in contrast to Arginine (which is mostly destroyed by your stomach and liver) it enters your blood intact. In fact, some studies have concluded that Citrulline is more effective in raising Arginine levels than supplementing with Arginine itself.

There are many possible forms of Citrulline, but the one I recommend is Citrulline Malate. It is this form that has been used in all of the research so far. The usual beneficial dosage for Citrulline is 8 grams a day. Many people prefer to take it before a workout; however, Nitric Oxide is mostly produced during your sleep, not around the time of your workout. It is recommended to be taken before sleep. In contrast, Arginine is not recommended to be taken before sleep because Arginine can suppress the endogenous production of Arginine. This is another reason why I recommend Citrulline over Arginine.

Many people use Citrulline together with BCAA and Creatine because Citrulline has been found to increase effects of BCAA (Branch Chained Amino Acids) and Creatine. To achieve a further synergy, Beta Alanine often accompanies Citrulline because Beta Alanine is different from Citrulline in buffering muscle fatigue. It also has other additional benefits.

Truth about Bodybuilding Supplements
Only for Professional Bodybuilders

RESUME

Citrulline is superior to Arginine, if you want to increase your NO balance for muscle growth. Additionally, Citrulline improves the effectiveness of Creatine and BCAAs.

The liver and stomach do not break down Citrulline. It enters directly into the blood.

The recommended Citrulline dosage is 8 grams a day usually taken before a workout. However, I recommend taking it before sleep because Nitric Oxide is mostly produced during sleep. In contrast to Arginine, supplementing Citrulline before sleep does not suppress the production of amino acids by the body.

A recommended stack is Citrulline, BCAA, Creatine and Beta Alanine. Alanine is sometimes excluded from the mix if taken before sleep because Alanine might disturb your sleep by causing the sensation of goose bumps.

BEETROOT

Beetroot is the prime source of Nitric Oxide, which triggers Anabolic muscle growth. Beetroot is naturally very high in nitrates. Additionally, it contains Betanin (which gives that red color to beetroots and it is an antioxidant), antioxidative Vitamins (which will additionally promote the longevity of Nitric Oxide in the body) and minerals including Sodium and Potassium, which you need during a workout to rehydrate yourself.

Beetroot supplements have many benefits. One of them is that they lower your blood pressure. Many stimulants are used in the sports industry that exhaust the hearts of bodybuilders. This puts them at the risk of heart attack. It is well known that intensive exercise puts extra pressure on your heart, so it is very wise to lower your blood pressure naturally. Lower blood pressure improves your Cardiovascular System - in a better system, the delivery of blood is more efficient during an exercise and more nutrients are carried to the muscles. Another benefit of Beetroot or any other Nitrate supplement is that it decreases the amount of Oxygen you need during a workout. Oxygen is used more effectively, thus you can lift heavier weights to shock your muscles into growth. If the Oxygen in your body is depleted (in simple words, no matter how hard you breathe you do not get enough Oxygen) during a workout then more Carbon Dioxide is accumulated and not removed soon enough. This leads to a spike of H+ (Hydrogen Ions) and

Lactic acid, which tire your muscles and switches your body into the catabolic state of disappearing muscles. You can improve your workout capacity by much as 20% using beetroot. Your Oxygen overall efficiency is improved by 11%. Add this to other supplements' effects and we are talking serious compounding numbers here.

Beetroot products are popular amongst professional sportsmen; however, if you drink a simple beetroot juice from a supermarket, you would have to consume 2 liters at the very least to gain any significant and immediate effect. Beetroot supplements are only worth the price if you are exercising extremely hard and the beetroot supplements you take are very concentrated. It is sensible to take it before a strenuous workout, about 15 to 30 minutes in advance. It will not remain in your body for long, but it will be used very quickly (it will last only for 90 minutes), so do not waste it. Use it only before a hard workout and to nudge your anabolic/catabolic inner scales into the anabolic positive. Common sense says that be prepared and do not be shocked if your excretion looks like a blood bath. This is because of Betanin, which is a very potent red colorant.

Still, after discovering all these fantastic benefits, the exact mechanism of the action is unknown at present. Some people theorize that the mechanism of action occurs through the dilation of blood. Because the mechanism is not known, the side effects of high dosages of Beetroot

Nitrate are also unknown variables. If you are purely after an NO boost then L-Arginine is a more money saving-supplement than Beetroot concentrate. However, if you can afford to buy Beetroot Concentrates for each gym session, it is a very good NO supplement choice because it is a powerful antioxidant and it provides Potassium and Sodium for hard workouts.

RESUME

Beetroot is a natural Nitric Oxide booster. It contains Nitrate which forms NO, Betanin – an antioxidant, and minerals, such as Sodium and Potassium, which help to replace electrolytes and rehydration and improve the Cardiovascular System and Oxygen use.

It is recommended to drink Beetroot 15 minutes before a workout and the effects of it last for 90 minutes.

BODYBUILDING SUPPLEMENTS AND SUBSTANCES TO AVOID

GLUCOSE, MALTODEXTRIN, FRUCTOSE ETC.

Many supplement companies add Dextrose, Glucose, Maltose, Maltodextrin, Sucrose and Lactose (milk sugar). All of them are forms of sugar. They cause an Insulin spike, and, by the way, Caffeine causes an Insulin spike as well. They need this spike because Insulin transports nutrients to the cells including muscle cells. However, this strategy is very dangerous at the very least. This method leads to Type 2 Diabetes. If you have Type 2 Diabetes, forget about bodybuilding. Of course, nothing is impossible and that is not to deter you from trying. It is extremely difficult to develop and maintain muscles with Type 2 Diabetes. Modern diet has plenty of refined sugars and caffeine. Before, 85 million people were registered with Type 2 Diabetes. In 2013, the number was registered at a whoping 347 million people, and there are many unknown cases. Additionally, Diabetes causes heart diseases, strokes, bad eyesight including blindness, and kidney illnesses. It even leads to amputation because of poor blood circulation.

The only time you can take sugar in relatively high amounts is immediately after a very strenuous workout. The effects are not as harmful because glucose stores are depleted in the muscles and your cells are ready to receive glucose made by your body from sugar.

To understand it further and motivate you against those poor fitness supplements that have too much sugar in them, we need to understand Diabetes and why we are in such great danger of getting it. By the way, it is just another example of fitness companies not having your interests at heart and just wanting your money without caring what happens to you.

There are two types of Diabetes. Type 1 Diabetes is a genetic illness. In Type 1 Diabetes, your pancreas stops producing Insulin. In my opinion, it is easier to cope with this type because Insulin is injected into your body. Many people might have the Diabetes gene, but it may never materialize. No matter how healthy or unhealthy you are, Type 1 Diabetes might just appear. Often it is provoked by bad reactions to some foods or common stress. Type 2 Diabetes is different as you can control it to avoid it. In Type 2 Diabetes, your cells including your precious muscle cells just ignore Insulin. Insulin transports nutrients such as Glucose, Protein and Fat into your blood cells. All of these nutrients are essential for life. Type 2 Diabetes is provoked by Insulin spikes caused by High GI foods, such as sugar, chocolate, ice-cream, white potatoes, alcohol, too much of white rice or white bread or white pasta. Mostly, anything carbohydrate based that is too refined. As mention in a previous chapter, High GI (High Glycemic Index) means your food is so refined that it is very easy for your body to process

the food just in half an hour. This leads to huge Insulin spikes, thus huge amounts of Glucose are produced and transported by Insulin into your cells. Insulin literally transports nutrients. Cells recognize the Insulin molecule and accept nutrients from it, but the cells do not need that large amount over such a short period. The cells begin to reject it. Over time the cells learn not to open to Insulin and consequentially do not receive nutrients. Imagine, an annoying telemarketer calling you every hour. You cannot differentiate between the call of the telemarketer and another person, thus you eventually ignore the calls. The same happens with your cells.

Type 2 Diabetes usually starts when cells reject Insulin carrying Glucose then they reject Insulin carrying protein and finally they reject Insulin carrying fats. Finally and utterly deadly, your cells do not receive any nutrients whatsoever and everything dies. In most cases, the fats are the last ones to be rejected. Often people with Type 2 Diabetes become fat before their death. Because it is notoriously hard to change lifestyles, the environment and habits, people with Type 2 Diabetes carry on eating unhealthy food. This sometimes speeds the progression of the illness.

That being said, do not go into another extreme and terrify yourself with a fear of sugar. Occasional Insulin spikes are fine, sensible amount of a sweet desert is also fine and High GI foods are even great straight after an intensive exercise because your Glycogen stores in your muscles need to be replenished for better recovery. Just make sure to look at your supplements and chose the ones without high levels of sugar or its forms except when it is a post workout supplement.

RESUME

Avoid supplements, which contain any type of derivative from sugar in big amounts to avoid Diabetes Type 2. The only time sugar is fine is straight after a strenuous workout.

Truth about Bodybuilding Supplements

Only for Professional Bodybuilders

CAFFEINE

Caffeine is very often advertised as a performance enhancer and, is used in many pre-workout supplements. Caffeine is also known as a thermogenic. It raises the body temperature and metabolic rate to burn more calories. Caffeine is not only in your coffee, it is also in your tea, in many pre-workout supplements and many fizzy drinks (the daddy of them all is the energy drink). Energy drinks are banned in some countries because of their addictive properties, adverse negative impact on high blood pressure and much more.

Some research also claims that caffeine helps to burn fat and preserve muscle because it increases the fatty acids from your fat reserves to burn them for energy instead of protein or carbohydrate. This, in turn, suppresses your appetite and you eat less. Although, this is most likely the truth and is proven by study after study, I am still not convinced because it is not the whole truth. You also need to know about caffeine's side effects, thus many health professionals, including doctors, are against caffeine. Some nutritionists might claim that even then caffeine is good in moderations as anything, but caffeine has a very nasty habit of breaking these moderations because it is highly addictive. Additionally, it is notoriously hard to control the amount of caffeine that we consume because it is in many products.

Nicotine also suppresses the appetite and slims you. Some might suggest that smoking one cigarette a day is useful for your health, but, because of its addictiveness, it is not the case. Caffeine exhausts the adrenal gland that produces adrenalin for your body. Caffeine is bad news for stressed people, especially in modern society. Most of all caffeine contributes towards the development of Type 2 Diabetes because Caffeine inflicts an Insulin spike. This illness means nutrients cannot be absorbed by your muscle cells making it virtually impossible to grow and maintain your muscles. Please read the chapter on Glucose for further information. One has to look at the positives and negatives of any supplement. In my opinion, the negatives of Caffeine outweigh the benefits.

Fitness products containing caffeine are easy to sell because caffeine is an addictive drug and it gives you that high which allows you to increase your efforts. If you are a supplement company, it is all good news because the customers buy cheap buzz, associate the buzz with the caffeine containing product and, best of all, these customers become addicted to it! Caffeine has many dangers e.g. high blood pressure that can simply kill you in many different ways. Caffeine stops the production of natural body antioxidants; as a result, you will age quicker. The sad truth is that around three cups of Coffee are sufficient to completely counteract all the supplements you take to aid the progress of your bodybuilding. Some research does indeed show performance enhancing qualities of caffeine for marathon runners. I want to

help bodybuilders, not runners, and caffeine is bad news for bodybuilders. Yes, one cup of coffee is fine and might be even good for a bodybuilder, but, because coffee is addictive, it is not always possible to be moderate, plus you have to consider Caffeine in everything e.g. cup of tea, coffee cake, carbonated drinks and, most dangerous, energy drinks. You might be just wasting money on enhancing supplements with too much Caffeine. As you are seriously in the business of growing your muscles in size, avoid Caffeine for at least this period. Boycotting Caffeine might take a lot of effort for some people, thus a gradual withdrawal of Caffeine is recommended. Of course, if you can do it in one go, please go ahead and do it.

Now let us have a further look at why Caffeine is so bad for a bodybuilder. The fact is that the relaxation of muscles is essential for bodybuilding. Power activities are all interplayed between relaxation and contraction of muscles. Our movements are operated through the mechanisms of the muscles' interplay. For example, during bicep curls, your biceps contract and your triceps relax. If both of them contracted, you arms would not move as your triceps would be pulling in one direction and your biceps would be pulling in the opposite direction. This principle applies to all skeletal muscles. Without coordinated relaxation and contraction of the opposing muscles, movement does not happen. An element responsible for the muscles' contraction and relaxation is Calcium. Calcium is stored deep inside your muscles. To tense a particular group of your muscles, Calcium is released to trigger contraction. As I mentioned before, the opposing muscles will need to relax to achieve this. Calcium is transported back into the muscles to relax them. Well, caffeine allows Calcium to escape out of your muscles. By doing so, enough Calcium is not available for the entire body and all of the bodybuilding activities are compromised.

Additionally, Caffeine is a diuretic as it provokes the body to quickly remove water. Muscle development is highly compromised when the muscles are dehydrated, so everything is halted.

The conclusion is avoid all the supplements, which contain caffeine if you are serious about building your muscles. Read labels carefully, especially on pre-workout supplements and fat burners. Yes, you will see contrary advice in many fitness magazines. As I mentioned before, it is easier for them to re-sell if you felt a caffeine kick and associated it with the product. Very conveniently for supplement companies, caffeine is highly addictive. Once you become addicted, subconsciously you will search for any positive opinion of caffeine, even if it is not scientific and you will disregard all the evidence against caffeine. Supplement companies do not even need to prove anything; you will prove it for them as any addict finds excuses and invalid justifications.

If you are only interested in slimming down, Caffeine might be suitable, but, because it is addictive, it compromises many natural body functions and increases the chances of a heart attack due to high blood pressure. I cannot recommend it even if all you are interested is slimming down.

RESUME

Caffeine is highly addictive and it is claimed to raise the body temperature, metabolic rate and burn fat.

However, the negative effects of Caffeine surpass all the positive effects by a large margin. Caffeine suppresses the adrenaline gland, promotes Type 2 Diabetes, causes high blood pressure, and stops the natural production of the body's antioxidants. Three cups of coffee are enough to counteract all of the positive benefits of most bodybuilding supplements. Caffeine encourages Calcium to escape from the muscles, thus the muscle's relaxation and development are compromised. Caffeine dehydrates the body pushing it into catabolic muscle eating state.

ALCOHOL

There were many studies on the impact of alcohol on bodybuilders. Alcohol interferes with the ability of the muscles to repair and grow. Alcohol halts proteins synthesis in your muscles, thus new muscles are not created. It particularly inhibits protein synthesis in Type 2 muscle fibers. This type of so called fast muscle fibers helps to lift heavy weights and makes you look muscular. Type 1 muscles fibers are responsible for cardio exercises like walking, running etc. Because alcohol is very destructive to your body, it pushes your body into a self-eating mode as your body literally breaks down your muscle tissues. Alcohol has a huge impact on your anabolic hormones. Due to alcohol your Testosterone levels become extremely low and you Growth Hormone levels are reduced as well. Alcohol interferes with your Insulin production by significantly decreasing its levels. A sufficient amount of Insulin is required to transport nutrients to your muscle cells or any other cells. Alcohol also creates huge amount of free radicals which are atoms missing an electron in their orbits. These atoms scavenge electrons from your cells by destroying them. This leads to further degradation of the body and halts your muscles recovery and growth. Alcohol slowly kills your liver which processes most of the stuff your body including your muscles need. Drinking too much? If the answer is yes, you can forget about that illusive six-pack right now.

Truth about Bodybuilding Supplements
Only for Professional Bodybuilders

However, let us be realistic. It is great for your bodybuilding goals if you simply do not drink and still manage to socialize well to keep your stress levels down and enjoy life. It is great if you are one of those rare people in the modern society. Most people find it impossible to avoid drinking. This book is not about alcoholism, the denial of it or the moderate consumption of it. Look for how we could negate some of the damage inflicted on us by alcohol, which includes the supplements discussed in this book e.g. Beta Alanine, Protein Powders, rehydration drinks etc. It is not to say, after drinking alcohol; you will be fine by dinking a magic potion. I am afraid the damage will still exist, albeit at a moderate amount.

RESUME

Alcohol prevents muscle repair and growth by dramatically reducing Insulin levels, increasing free radicals, which destroy the body, and suppressing your hormones etc. In particular, it almost stops muscle growth and repair in Type 2 Muscles, which gives you a muscular physique.

Because of the destruction by alcohol, the body switches into a catabolic state during which the muscles are eaten for energy.

This book is not about alcoholism, but moderation and readiness, hence look for how we could negate some of the damage inflicted on us by alcohol. Consider the supplements discussed in this book e.g. Beta Alanine, Protein Powders, rehydration drinks etc.

TRIBULUS

Tribulus is a weed that grows in warm regions and is best known as Tribulus Terrestris. It is commonly believed to raise Testosterone levels and came to us from the Chinese and Indian schools of supplementation. However, authoritative studies are not available to confirm that it raises Testosterone levels.

Bodybuilders who use Testosterone boosting steroids often use Tribulus. These bodybuilders use it after their cycle of Testosterone steroids. These steroids are believed to suppress the natural production of Testosterone after the end of supplementation. Tribulus is used to repair that by trying to revive the natural production of Testosterone. Other bodybuilders use it without steroids.

The effectiveness of Tribulus was tested on some animals. This test has demonstrated an increase in Testosterone levels; however, another research on young men demonstrated that Testosterone did not increase in them. Tribulus has also been known to increase the levels of Dihydrotestosterone (DHT) and Dehydroepiandrosterone (DHEA). DHT is a sex steroid and promotes good sexual health. DHEA is one of the most abundant steroid hormones in a human. It helps with the synthesis of sex hormones in humans. Note here that it is one of the most abundant steroids in the human body, hence there is no urgent need to supplement it.

To conclude, save your money and buy something else. It is just hype now and it is an expensive hype. So far, human studies have proven the ineffectiveness of Tribulus on bodybuilders.

RESUME

Tribulus is a weed from warm climates. It is claimed to increase Testosterone levels in a human. However, authoritative studies have not confirmed that it raises testosterone levels in humans.

TESTOFEN ALSO KNOWN AS FENUSIDE, FENUTEST ETC.

I decided to discuss this supplement in short to demonstrate the useless marketing that is online and in health stores. Testofen's main ingredient is essentially a simple herb used for cooking - it is called Fenugreek!

I visited a website on which a study of Testofen (Fenugreek) on 60 healthy adult men is mentioned. The study demonstrated a significant increase in Testosterone levels. Only at the end of the article after marketing Testofen, it is mentioned that the Testofen (Fenugreek) was also accompanied by Zinc, Magnesium and Vitamin B6, which were "added for vitamin and mineral support". Oh, really? Just for "Vitamin and mineral support"? A combination of Zinc, Magnesium and B6 is known as ZMA, which works independently as discussed in the chapter on ZMA. They might as well have added Testosterone injectable steroids to Testofen and write that "steroids were added for vitamin support due to a high spike of Testosterone induced by Testofen".

Have a further look at how it was marketed; it was called Testo (hinting Testosterone) and then this "magical" Fen follows (sounds like Feng Shui, a Chinese system following the laws of the Heaven and Earth). However it is a simple fenugreek herb – buy it from your local supermarket and use it for cooking.

There are some benefits of Fenugreek. It fends of colds, it is an antioxidant, it claims to increase a Growth Hormone (that is so low in adult humans that even quadrupling does not show a significant benefit) and it seems to be a "fix it all elixir". I hope I made my point clear. Do not waste your money on it and save your money for other scientifically proven bodybuilding supplements, which can be expensive, thus save that cash by not buying hyped supplements.

This chapter on Testofen is written for you to show why you should not trust just any health supplement claiming to be good for bodybuilders. There are so many of them that it is insane to mention them all here. Use this chapter as your guide and always try to find valid research supporting the claims, and most of all read the research to see if it is valid and not manipulated. In any case, this book on bodybuilding supplements covers all that you need as a bodybuilder.

RESUME

Testofen is just an ordinary Fenugreek. You can find it in most supermarkets. It is claimed to increase Testosterone levels, but this is a false claim. It is just a poorly researched antioxidant and over-marketed supplement.

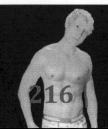

ALLI ALSO KNOWN AS ORLISTAT OR XENICAL

Alli is one of the recent supplements, which has taken drug and supplements stores by storm. Alli, thanks to an ingredient called "Orlistat", blocks 25% of fat from being absorbed by your body. Alli is bad news for a bodybuilder because you need good fats for your proper development. Saturated fats are good for you, Essential Fats are called so for a reason - they are essential. Omega 3, Omega 6 and Omega 9 are all fats and necessary for your body. Your body also needs crucial fat-soluble Vitamins and Alli is bad news for them. Did you know that Testosterone molecules are made of fat? The only fats that are bad are Trans Fats that clog your system which are banned in some parts of the World. Many recommend wearing dark underwear while on Alli because it can cause "leakages".

Alli reduces your calorie intake. Dieting and losing weight relies on burning more calories through the day than the calories you consume. Blocking good fats that are essential for your body compromises your muscle growth. It is like reducing cement to glue bricks together when you are building your house. There is no substitute to a sensible diet that provides all the nutrients, exercise and sufficient calorie deficit if your goal is to lose weight. While losing weight, it is a good idea to supplement with HMB to retain your muscle tissues. Read the chapter on HMB for further information.

Fat is not the biggest issue in the modern diet, but highly processed Carbohydrates, also known as High Glycemic Index (High GI), are the biggest issue. These Carbohydrates have to be used in half an hour after consumption for energy or they are converted and stored as fat. High GI Carbohydrates have so many calories in them that not all of the calories can be used for energy over such a short period. In opposition, there are Low GI Carbohydrates that can be burnt for energy up to four hours after consumption, thus your body has plenty of chances to utilize them. High GI Carbohydrates can only be taken by bodybuilders immediately after a strenuous workout to replace Glycogen stores in your muscles to prevent catabolism. This is the only time you can indulge in chocolate or ice cream and do something good for your body. Of course, this should be in moderation, just enough to replenish your Glycogen stores.

Alli is very expensive and is bad for a bodybuilder as it costs too much. Hire a health nutritionist or a personal trainer instead.

RESUME

Alli blocks 25% of fat absorption; however, it is bad because it blocks essential fats, which are necessary for health and muscle development. Alli might cause uncontrolled diarrhea. It is not fat, but High GI foods that are the main problem in a modern diet.

CARBOHYDRATES BLOCKERS

There are so many brands of Carbohydrates blockers that this book would not be enough to describe them all. All of them have one common feature; they block Carbohydrates. These Carbohydrates are essential for a healthy life. Some people think that, because Carbohydrates are a problem, they should be blocked. They do not know that Hi GI Carbohydrates are the problem. Other Carbohydrates are fantastic and they reduce general acidity in the body. Acidity causes your body to switch into a catabolic state during which your body eats itself including the hard earned muscles.

Some of the Carbohydrates blockers are based on an extract from kidney beans, which block Low GI Carbohydrates from being absorbed. This is bad for anyone who wants to stay healthy, including bodybuilders who want to stay healthy. In any case, some studies show that modern carbohydrate blockers do not have enough of the kidney bean extract in them to block sufficiently.

We all live on Carbohydrates. They are our main energy source that keeps us alive. They provide essential nutrients without which hormone production is compromised. It is all about how you program yourself to eat. If your do not train yourself to eat well even if you do lose weight, you will without a doubt put it all back very quickly. If you decide to supplement with

Carbohydrates Blockers from time to time, you will slowly compromise you muscle growth because high levels of energy are absent, your body becomes body acidic and your body lacks nutrient,

RESUME

Carbohydrates should not be blocked as they are essential for keeping you energetic and keeping nutrients in the body and maintaining an anabolic muscle-growing environment. Change your eating habits for proper results.

THERMOGENIC SUPPLEMENTS

Thermogenic supplements are supposed to burn fat by increasing your body temperature, which in turn increases your metabolism. However, if you think the ingredients are only designed in laboratories, it is not so. The ingredients that increase temperatures are as simple as caffeine, cinnamon, green tea, bitter orange, mustard, ginger, and different varieties of chilies, especially cayenne. Green tea contains caffeine, which increases the body temperature. Cinnamon is often added to Thermogenic supplements because it drastically increases the burning rate of cell sugars and encourages Insulin use so that a sugar spike is avoided and the heart remains healthy. One of the properties of bitter orange is that it suppresses appetite. Only a small amount of research has been done on bitter orange so the claims are just speculations at the moment. A concentrated extract of bitter orange is considered life threatening as it causes high blood pressure, an irregular heartbeat, heart attacks, strokes and finally death. Aspirin is often added because, according to some studies, it increases the Thermogenic response. Aspirin also thins the blood, which increases the heat resistance of the body and lengthens its impact. Still why should you use expensive Thermogenic when you can just spice up what your are cooking or have your steak with three times more mustard or horseradish. Besides, coffee is an absolute enemy of bodybuilders. Please read the chapter on Caffeine to find out why.

Yes, some ingredients are good for you if you gain them from food. Undoubtedly, Caffeine and a concentrated extract of bitter orange are harmful for you. Avoid Caffeine and a too concentrated extract of bitter orange and you might be able to help yourself lose that stubborn fat to really show all the muscle definition.

RESUME

Thermogenics increase the body temperature and heart rate. Caffeine and a highly concentrated extract of bitter orange should be avoided because of the related health risks. It is best to cook Thermogenics with mustard, ginger, different varieties of chilies, cinnamon and natural bitter orange.

CREATING AN ANABOLIC ENVIRONMENT

Before moving on in this chapter, let us clearly define an Anabolic Environment. The opposite of an Anabolic environment is a Catabolic environment. In a Catabolic state, your body scavenges your muscles for food and uses most of the proteins, hormones, vitamins, mineral etc. which are meant for your muscles. The result is simple to understand; your muscles reduce in size or stagnate no matter what you do, how hard you exercise, what you eat and what supplements you take. The Catabolic environment is caused by many factors. Some of them are over-exercising, under eating, alcohol, depression etc. In an Anabolic environment your muscles easily grow because there is enough stimulus, not too much or too little, because plenty of nutrients are provided by your body to your muscles and because hormone play is in your favor, thus you have extra Testosterone and other hormones.

These two environments are not black and white and are not something, which happens over minutes. You enter into an Anabolic state by following the right method. If you had a heavy drinking session last weekend, it will take some time, if not weeks to return to an Anabolic state.

Creating an Anabolic environment is not limited to how hard and how often you workout or what supplements you take. The good news is that you

create an Anabolic state and you are in the driving seat. A major part of it is to know about the different types of exercises that influence your body in the most effective way. One of the biggest parts of it is what you put into your body. Yes, it is true, although you cannot believe all the advertisements in the fitness magazines, but most of them are truthful in how much they were surprised to find out that diet creates an Anabolic environment. Supplements also influence the Anabolic environment but to a lesser degree, unless you are taking steroids. Taking steroids prevents you from gaining the fruits of professional bodybuilding where you are paid for doing what you love, such as various bodybuilding competitions, advertising, great health etc. Because this book is about supplements, we will have a look at the influence of supplements on the Anabolic environment. I have mentioned that it is a lesser part in comparison to Diet and Exercise, which I hope to cover in one of my future books, but in a professional sport it is those last seconds that make you the greatest winner. It is those milliliters and eights of an inch that make you stand out. It is a shorter time for muscle recovery. It is that extra ability to lift weights. Then, through accumulative and compounding power, you tip the scales in favor of an Anabolic state

Oversupplementing before a workout is not a good idea, if it is anything more than a small supplement of Vitamin C and Beta Alanine, Nitric Oxide (NO) booster, and of course, water. Do not take Caffeine at any time. Read the chapter on Caffeine to understand why. If you oversupplement before a workout you can feel bloated and your food is not properly digested because you are moving. Consuming anything before a workout actually reduces your energy. This is because, to consume anything, your body has to first digest it, and to digest, your body needs energy, which competes for the energy for the workout. Additionally, most supplements are not effective immediately, but reach their effective levels in the body over an extended period. Once you have reached these levels, the supplements do not just disappear all of a sudden e.g. Creatine, ZMA etc. Many supplements compete for vital resources which you need during your workout e.g. Creatine needs plenty of water, so does your workout. In a state of dehydration, your performance is badly affected. Dehydration is one of the leading causes for your body to return into a state of Catabolic muscle destruction or plateau.

The best time to supplement for most of the supplements is immediately after an exercise. Of course, this is a generalization with many exceptions e.g. it is best to take ZMA one hour before sleep followed by Casein Protein and Citrulline at least half an hour later. Generally, post workout is the best period to supplement because after your strenuous efforts your muscle cells are at the most sensitive state to Insulin. They open up more willingly when they feel the presence of Insulin carrying nutrients to them. You have to take full advantage of this metabolic window of opportunity. This is the

only time High GI like sugars is good for you. This is also the time to take Protein Powders. Protein Powders stimulate Insulin in a safer way than just sugars. The compounded muscle sensitivity to Insulin and increased stimulation of Insulin without bad consequences generally means that whatever you add to your sugars (Carbohydrates) and protein mix will be absorbed properly and faster by your muscle cells.

All of this excitement in the body has a very positive effect on the hormones, which are needed for rapid muscle growth. Proteins with carbohydrates are highly anabolic after a workout. If you are not feeding your body with proper supplements and food, you are wasting most of your effort. Yes, your muscles recover to some degree whilst sleeping during which Casein protein powder is useful, but the effect of the right foods and supplements on the anabolic state is greater and better after a workout. Once your body is correctly fed, your muscles will recover more during your sleep. Starving your body immediately after a workout will badly affect your body, which will enter into a catabolic state. Your amino acids (different types of protein) are depleted, your glucose reserves are depleted and everything comes under great stress. This inevitably will lead to your body entering the Catabolic state. It is at this point, more than any other, that you can say good bye to your muscles if you do not correctly feed and supplement your body. It does not matter what and how well you did in the gym, you just wasted your time. "Congratulations", by starving your body, it decided to cannibalize itself.

By the way, because of this depletion, it is highly recommended not to exercise for more than 50 minutes and to give an absolute minimum of 4 hours between workouts. This allows for the body to recover while you are giving your body nutrients during these four hours.

If you do not accomplish much in the 50 minute period, or you do not constantly sweat and are not often out of breath in the gym and you want to be a serious bodybuilder, then you are confusing a gym with a social club or a relaxing parlor. One of the great methods is to buy a heart rate monitor and never allow your heart to beat less than 125 - 130 beats a minute. If it does then your body has had a sufficient short break between sets and it is time to get back to your workout.

After a workout, it is important to have carbohydrates and proteins. Usually, the recommendation is a minimum of 2 portions of Carbohydrates for each portion of protein. Obviously, you need protein, but you must eat Carbohydrates too as they contain fiber for digestion and absorption, essential vitamins and elements. They are the main energy source for the body.

Another crucial piece of advice is that you have to feed your body regularly and frequently by eating small portions every 3 hours. This will increase your metabolism and muscle growth. We are designed this way from the ice age; eat and eat regularly to convince your body that there is plenty of food, convince it to stay anabolic, avoid storing fat and avoid the catabolic state.

RESUME

The Anabolic state encourages muscle growth. The Catabolic state is the opposite state. A Catabolic environment is the result of poor diet and exercise, overconsumption of alcohol, depression and overexercising.

Before an exercise, it is better to supplement as little as possible to avoid a reduction in energy due to the digestion of most muscle-building supplements. The most suitable time to supplement is straight after a workout. It is a crucial time to supplement or your body will switch to a catabolic state. After a workout is the correct time to take High GI carbs to replace the muscles' glycogen. It is best to take low digesting and hormone stimulating supplements before sleep because the body repairs itself during sleep.

Avoid exercising more than 50 minutes to avoid entering the Catabolic state. Keep your heart rate above 125 – 130 beats per minute during a workout. Eat 2 portions of Carbohydrates to 1 portion of protein. Every 3 hours, eat small potions.

Truth about Bodybuilding Supplements

Only for Professional Bodybuilders

GOOD LUCK AND BE MUSCULAR!

Sincerely,

Serge Kolpa

Now that you know the Truth about Bodybuilding Supplements you can supercharge your progress. If you have a question or two then come to my website www.fitserko.com, specifically created for this book, there is a Bodybuilding forum where you can ask your questions. There you can find where is the best bodybuilding supplements online store in your geographical area. I personally research the online stores and then offer you what is the best. See you there… www.fitserko.com

BE MUSCULAR

Serge Kolpa

Printed in Great Britain
by Amazon.co.uk, Ltd.,
Marston Gate.